Hedda Gabler
Sirens: Elektra
in Bosnia

Also by Judith Thompson

Body & Soul
The Crackwalker
Enoch Arden in the Hope Shelter
Habitat
Lion in the Streets
Palace of the End
Perfect Pie
Such Creatures
The Thrill
Watching Glory Die
White Biting Dog and Other Plays

Hedda Gabler
Sirens: Elektra
in Bosnia

Judith Thompson

Playwrights Canada Press
Toronto

For professional or amateur production rights, please contact:
Rena Zimmerman, Great North Artists Management
350 Dupont Street, Toronto, ON M5R 1V9
416.925.2051, renazimmerman@gnaminc.com

Library and Archives Canada Cataloguing in Publication
[Plays. Selections]
        Hedda Gabler ; &, Sirens : Elektra in Bosnia / Judith Thompson.
-- First edition.

Adaptations of Hedda Gabler by Henrik Ibsen, and Electra by Sophocles.
Contents: Hedda Gabler -- Sirens : Elektra in Bosnia.
Issued in print and electronic formats.
ISBN 978-1-77091-754-5 (softcover).--ISBN 978-1-77091-755-2 (PDF).--
ISBN 978-1-77091-756-9 (HTML).--ISBN 978-1-77091-757-6 (Kindle)

    I. Sophocles. Electra. II. Ibsen, Henrik, 1828-1906. Hedda Gabler.
III. Thompson, Judith, 1954- . Hedda Gabler. IV. Thompson, Judith,
1954- . Sirens. V. Title. VI. Title: Sirens : Elektra in Bosnia. VII. Title:
Plays. Selections.

PS8589.H4883A6 2017   C812'.54   C2017-901351-3
                                            C2017-901352-1

We acknowledge the financial support of the Canada Council for the Arts, the Ontario Arts Council (OAC), the Ontario Media Development Corporation, and the Government of Canada for our publishing activities.

 Canada Council Conseil des arts
for the Arts du Canada

 ONTARIO ARTS COUNCIL
CONSEIL DES ARTS DE L'ONTARIO
an Ontario government agency
un organisme du gouvernement de l'Ontario

 Canada  Ontario
Ontario Media Development
Corporation

Foreword
by Cynthia Ashperger

In *Hedda Gabler* and *Sirens: Elektra in Bosnia*, Judith Thompson has undertaken the daunting task of adapting two dramatic masterpieces: Henrik Ibsen's realist classic and Aeschylus's trilogy of Greek tragedies, *The Oresteia*. I was fortunate enough to have performed in both of these adaptations, and working in Judith's presence was a very human, surprising, and uncompromising experience. But then again, summing up the experience of working with Judith Thompson is impossible. Her work is deep, poetic, surrealistic, exciting, and large. She reaches for the subjects that are uncomfortable and inconvenient, digging under the surface of issues, where we are all equally bloody.

Judith's *Hedda* stays close to the original, but distinguishes itself through the title character's motivation, which goes well beyond being entrapped in her husband's powers. During rehearsals Judith introduced the possibility of her Hedda having been abused as a child and experiencing self-hatred because of that unresolved past. Hedda's past of self-hatred builds throughout the play to the point of release in a public, violent act of protest, and not one that occurs backstage as in the original. The streamlined and poetic language of this adaptation carries the actors' imaginations. And this is why I personally fall in love with Judith's writing over and over again. I don't have to "work" her metaphors and images. They simply carry me, one to the next, providing me with an inner monologue that furnishes the logic of a character.

Sirens: Elektra in Bosnia is a masterful adaptation in that it synthesizes Aeschylus's trilogy—*Agamemnon, The Libation Bearers,* and *The Eumenides*—into one play. While the production of *Hedda* that I performed in was set in modern-day Canada as interpreted by director Ross Manson, Judith herself chose to move *Sirens* to the present. The Trojan War becomes the wars in Yugoslavia: Menelaus and Agamemnon fight on opposite sides as two Bosnian-Serbian brothers; Agamemnon is married to a Muslim Clytemnestra and fights for the pro-Yugoslav forces, while his brother has chosen the side of the brutal paramilitary soldiers fighting for greater Serbia; and Iphigenia is the child of a pre-civil-war Bosnian mixed marriage. But the starring turn is Elektra's, who narrates the play through flashbacks, revealing the jealous motivations that lead her to murder. And it is this very human, deep-seated jealousy that Judith constructs as "the cause" of the family's demise. The cause of an entire war in Judith's *Elektra* comes from a secret hatred held deep within, and that sin of hatred is strong enough to set destruction in motion. Hatred in one heart spreads like wildfire.

In *Hedda* I played Berthe, and in *Elektra* I was Clytemnestra. When I think of Berthe, I think of a little gem of role. Judith expands it from the original and gives her keen and loving attention, and she gives her some space as the only lower-class character in that play. Judith's Clytemnestra is a complex character whose journey is one of grief and loss. Her first speech, one of unconditional love as she laments over her dead daughter, is beautiful and unforgettable. It still sometimes reverberates in my mind and in itself encompasses the greatness of Judith's writing: her depth of compassion, her ability to enter a character's psyche, her penchant for magic realism, her beautiful poetry, and the immense size of her drama.

Dr. Cynthia Ashperger was born in Zagreb, Croatia, where she had extensive experience in the theatre, film, and television industries as an actor. She holds a Ph.D. from University of Toronto's Graduate Centre for Studies in Drama. She has taught acting at Ryerson Theatre School since 1994, where she is also the director of acting program. She lives in Toronto, where she also works as an acclaimed director, writer, actor, and producer.

Hedda Gabler

Hedda Gabler was first produced by the Shaw Festival at the Court House Theatre, Niagara-on-the-Lake, from August 8 to September 22, 1991, with the following cast and creative team:

Hedda Gabler: Fiona Reid
Eilert Lovborg: Jim Mezon
Aunt Juliana: Joan Orenstein
Berthe: Ann Holloway
George Tesman: Derek Boyes
Thea Elvsted: Sharry Flett
Judge Brack: Roger Rowland
Manservant: Matthew Henry
Manservants: Robin Avery and Peter Wilds

Director: Judith Thompson
Designer: Cameron Porteous
Lighting Designer: Ereca Hassell
Stage Manager: Charlotte Green
Assistant Stage Manager: Jennifer Johnston
Original music composed by Bill Thompson in consultation with Yuval R. Fichman

An expanded version of the play was produced by Volcano Theatre, Toronto, in 2005 with the following cast and creative team:

Starring: Cynthia Ashperger, Ann Baggley, Tanja Jacobs, Tom McCamus, Yanna McIntosh, Alon Nashman, and Nigel Shawn Williams

Director: Ross Manson
Set and Costumes Designer: Teresa Przybylski
Sound Designer: John Gzowksi
Lighting Designer: Bonnie Beecher

Characters

Aunt J
Berthe
Eilert Lovborg
George Tesman
Hedda Gabler
Judge Brack
Thea Elvsted

Act One

Moonlight fills a large drawing room, furnished in nineteenth-century upper-middle class style, with dark colours. In the rear wall is a broad, open doorway with curtains drawn back to either side. It leads to a smaller room. Above the sofa is a painted portrait of a handsome old man in a general's uniform. There are flowers on every surface.

The music suggests a frantic, dark dream of freedom.

HEDDA Gabler, a vital young woman of twenty-nine, appears in her nightgown, barefoot, and dances an expressionistic, wild dance. The dance shows her intense desire for freedom and ecstasy.

This dance is actually what HEDDA is dreaming in her bedroom close by. It is a dream of freedom. HEDDA disappears as suddenly as she appeared.

Dawn breaks. AUNT J—Juliana Tesman—a single lady of sixty-five and of pleasant appearance, enters holding flowers, with BERTHE, an older maid, large and plain looking. AUNT J surveys the room, singing a traditional romantic song called "She Moved Through The Fair." AUNT J wears a new hat and holds a parasol. She gives the flowers to BERTHE as she enters. BERTHE takes them off stage to find a vase.

AUNT J: "And this she did say: It will not be long love till our wedding day."

AUNT J curtseys to the painting of the general and continues to sing:

"I dreamed it last night that my true love came in
So softly he entered his feet made no din
He came close beside me and this he did say
'It will not be long, love, till our wedding day.' "

BERTHE enters with the flowers in a vase.

BERTHE: Jesus, Mary, and Joseph, will ya keep it down. She'll have our heads!

AUNT J: *(gasps)* Good gracious, do you mean they're still sleeping then?

BERTHE: Yes, miss, I toldja, the boat didn't get in till midnight. I toldja that.

AUNT J: On my goodness.

BERTHE: And didn't I have to be up till three in the morning unpacking for her? She was standing right over me the whole time.

AUNT J: Oh well they must sleep then. We'll be quiet as mice. And I know, let's fill the room with nice, fresh air for them when they wake up.

BERTHE: Gracious, I don't know where to put these flowers—every inch is covered—look at that. I'll have to put them on the piano; do you think she'll mind?

AUNT J: Oh, Berthe, it will be strange for you to have a new mistress. It is very hard to let you go, you know.

BERTHE: How do you think it is for me, miss? After all the happy years I spent with you and Miss Rina? Eh? Eh?

AUNT J: Please come and sit down, Berthe. Let's talk.

BERTHE: No, I don't want to sit down.

AUNT J: Berthe, please, you must know that I'm stomach sick about your leaving us, truly sick about it, after thirty-nine years? It's like . . . It's like . . .

BERTHE: Well then, I'm not stayin' here. I'm goin' back with youse, like it or not.

AUNT J: But Georgie needs you, dear. He has since he was a baby.

BERTHE: That new maid you got is a slug. She don't know how to take care of Rina.

AUNT J: I . . . shall take care of Rina—are you saying that I can't take care of my own sister?

BERTHE: I'M SAYING . . . I'm saying that Hedda Gabler don't find me to her liking, that's the feeling I get.

AUNT J: *Mrs. Tesman*, Berthe; she belongs to George now. Mrs. Tesman, if you please.

BERTHE: Well whoever she is she treats me like horse plop.

AUNT J: Remember who you are, Berthe. She happens to be the daughter of General Gabler. She is your BETTER, she is MY better—

BERTHE: Better at what?

AUNT J: THINK of the life, Berthe; think of the life she had when the general was alive, almost like royalty? As long as I LIVE I'll never forget the sight of her and her father riding by every night on that gigantic dark horse? In the long black skirt . . . flowing in the wind, and, and . . . the feather! Do you remember that fire-red feather that stuck straight up from her hat—

BERTHE: Feather?

AUNT J: Berthe, whatever you may think, you must show her respect; she is our Georgie's wife. He's very lucky to have her and she's a catch.

TESMAN enters with an empty travelling bag.

BERTHE: Poor Georgie-bookworm—I don't think he knows what he's caught—

AUNT J: Dr. Tesman, Berthe; that's another thing, you must always address him as Dr. Tesman, now, NOT Georgie; you musn't ever call him—

TESMAN jumps into view.

TESMAN: Berty can call me anything she wants, can't you, Berty?

BERTHE: Hello there, Georgie.

TESMAN and BERTHE hug.

Let me take those for you now.

BERTHE takes books from TESMAN as they hug, then puts a photo album on the desk.

TESMAN: Hullo, Auntie Julioo, what a wonderful—

BERTHE exits with the books.

AUNT J: I—didn't wake you, did I, George? You see Berthe didn't tell that you were—

TESMAN: Auntie, I'm just tickled to see your lovely old face! *(sings)* "Oh Mia Cara."

AUNT J: *(whispering)* George! Perhaps we shouldn't.

TESMAN: Hey, did you get home from the harbour all right? I just felt awful about leaving you there!

AUNT J: Oh, nonsense! There wasn't space enough for a flea left in your carriage, dear!

TESMAN: With all Hedda's luggage—true enough! But still—

AUNT J: That nice Judge Brack took me home, George; don't you worry a bit.

TESMAN: Come here, *(takes AUNT J to sofa)* let's sit down and have a chitty-chat. Come on! There. Let me untie your bonnet for you . . .

> *BERTHE enters with a water jug and two glasses. TESMAN removes AUNT J's hat.*

Ohhhhh it's a pretty bonnet.

He puts the hat on his head.

It's new, isn't it?

AUNT J: I bought it for Hedda!

TESMAN: For Hedda!

AUNT J: So she wouldn't think I was a frump! If we went out on a walk together.

TESMAN: "Most perspicacious!"

AUNT J: George! You and your big words—

TESMAN: Auntie J, tell me, I didn't get a chance to ask you last night, with all the excitement, how is Auntie Rina? I've been so worried, you know, the whole honeymoon—

AUNT J: Well, George, she is . . . dying. I have to face that. I only hope that . . . God lets me keep her a while longer . . . I . . . When I lose her I just don't know what I'll do! I'll be a useless bag of bones—

TESMAN: Julioo! Please . . . don't . . .

AUNT J: Oh, George, I am so happy for you—catching Hedda Gabler, imagine! The most beautiful, admired—

TESMAN: I hear every man in town is frothing at the mouth with jealousy—

AUNT J: And such a lovely long honeymoon! So—romantic!

TESMAN: Six months of the most serious and gratifying academic research I've done, Auntie, honestly—

AUNT J: George, come on, do you have any news? Marvellous news?

TESMAN: Well—you know of course that I received my doctorate—

AUNT J: Yes, oh yes, but I mean . . . aren't you maybe expecting something?

TESMAN: Expecting what?

AUNT J: After all, George, I'm practically your mother.

TESMAN: The professorship! Oh yes, I expect to be given that, Auntie J, VERY soon.

AUNT J: That's . . . wonderful, George—it will certainly be helpful in . . . covering your . . . costs—

TESMAN: Yes, I suppose a mansion like this is expensive. How much do you think it—

AUNT J: Well, we won't know, dear, until we see the bills.

TESMAN: Judge Brack said in his letter, though, that he got it on very good terms.

AUNT J: And I've given a guarantee for all the furniture and appointments, so you don't have to—

TESMAN: What? What kind of—

AUNT J: From our nest egg, dear. We were delighted to help—

TESMAN: But. But . . . that's all that you and Rina have—

AUNT J: Well, George, Judge Brack said it would be very helpful—

TESMAN: But—Auntie—no—

AUNT J: It's just a formality, really, and, anyway, starting soon you'll have your professor money coming in and everything will be just fine. Don't worry about us.

TESMAN: Your nest egg! Oh, it's imperative that I get that post immediately, immediately.

AUNT J: Well, George, you only have one possible rival.

TESMAN: You think they might give it to him? To Eilert Lovborg?

AUNT J: Give that . . . werewolf a professorship? In the university? No, no, George, he may have written a book, but he's still Eilert Lovborg, and his reputation is in tatters—oh no I don't think he'll be standing in your way again.

TESMAN: A book? What book has he—

AUNT J: I'm sure it's nothing but a scribble compared to the one you're working on, George. What is *your* book—

TESMAN: Medieval—uh . . . domestic industries in . . . ancient uh—France, Auntie.

AUNT J: Ohhh it sounds spellbinding, spellbinding!

BERTHE enters and dusts the piano keys.

TESMAN: Actually, I'd better get to work on it right now. Oh—I've got so much to do! Such a huge amount of . . .

AUNT J: I'm sure you'll finish it in a matter of weeks, Georgie.

TESMAN: Working in this . . .

HEDDA enters.

. . . wonderful home.

BERTHE watches HEDDA from the back room.

AUNT J: With your . . . beautiful . . . new bride.

TESMAN: Oh yes, Julioo, yes, yes, you know I think she's the most wonderful woman in the entire . . .

He sees HEDDA and stands up.

Hedda!

AUNT J: Good morning.

AUNT J stands up and curtsies, hat in hand.

Hedda, my dear! How are you, good morning!

HEDDA: Good morning, Miss Tesman. How lovely to see you with the morning light. Please do sit.

HEDDA notices that the dust covers have not yet been removed. Horrified, she removes all of them.

AUNT J: Oh! Well, thank you . . . Did the uh . . . new bride sleep well in the uh . . . ex-prime minister's widow's old mansion?

HEDDA: *(preoccupied)* What was that? Did you say something?

AUNT J: Did you . . . sleep well, dear?

HEDDA: Ohhh no, I had a most turbulent night, thank you.

TESMAN: Turbulent? You were sleeping like an old cat when I woke up!

He snores in imitation.

HEDDA: How fortunate for me.

HEDDA hands all the dust covers to BERTHE.

Brigitte, darling, I never want to see these again. This is not a mausoleum.

BERTHE: Very well, madam.

TESMAN: That's Berthe, dearest.

BERTHE exits with the armload of dust covers.

HEDDA: Thank you, Berthe! You see, Miss Tesman, I always find that new surroundings . . . impede peaceful slumber, don't you?

AUNT J: Oh yes, I know exactly what you mean. When Rina and I travelled to—

HEDDA: Does anybody else find it too bright in here? It's terribly, terribly bright, isn't it? . . . Tesman, quick, quickly, the room is flooded with sunlight—

TESMAN runs to close the curtains.

AUNT J: Oh poor dear Hedda, let me close the curtains for you—

TESMAN starts to close the window and curtains.

HEDDA: No! Please! Tesman, LEAVE THE WINDOWS open. Do you want me to suffocate?

TESMAN: All right!

HEDDA: I need air, Tesman, air.

TESMAN: There we are, Hedda. Shade and fresh air. How's that? Is that better?

HEDDA: Somewhat. Oh yes, that air is much better, especially with all these fragrant flowers! Miss Tesman, please, do sit down—can I offer you some—refreshment, some Turkish delight? Or—

AUNT J: Oh thank you, dear; I wouldn't dream of keeping you. I just wanted to make sure you were settled in.

AUNT J starts to go.

TESMAN: Give Rina all my love, Julioo, and tell her I'll be over to see her this afternoon.

AUNT J: Oh! George! I almost forgot!

TESMAN: What? What is it, Auntie?

AUNT J: Here you are, dear.

She hands him a package.

TESMAN: Auntie, you saved them for me! Oh! I can't tell you how much this means to me, honestly . . .

He turns to HEDDA.

Hedda—

HEDDA: What is it?

TESMAN: My old slippers! Can you believe it?

HEDDA: They look like two old rats run over by a carriage! I'm joking, Miss Tesman. I know these are very precious to Tesman—he talked of them constantly on our honeymoon.

TESMAN: A couple of old friends, really. Look, Hedda, see how Auntie Rina has embroidered them for me? Even though she was so sick? They bring back so many memories—look, Hedda!

HEDDA: They don't bring back any for me. GET them away from me!

AUNT J: George, please, Hedda might not—

HEDDA: Tesman, that maid must go.

AUNT J: Berthe? What—

TESMAN: Why, dear? Why do you—

HEDDA: Well she's left her old hat on the sofa.

TESMAN: Hedda!

HEDDA: What if someone came in and saw it? Sitting there like a . . . running sore . . .

TESMAN: Hedda, it's—

AUNT J: No!

TESMAN: Aunt Juliana's hat.

HEDDA: Oh. Is it?

AUNT J: Yes, I'm afraid it is. And it's . . . not . . . old . . . at all, actually.

HEDDA: Is it not?

AUNT J: In fact, it's the first time I've ever worn it.

TESMAN: It's just . . . beautiful, really, *très, très élégant*.

AUNT J: Oh no, George, it's very ordinary. Now where's my parasol! Ah. This is mine too. Not . . . Berthe's.

TESMAN: A new hat and a new parasol—look, Hedda, aren't they lovely?

HEDDA: Very nice.

TESMAN: You see, Julioo, Hedda just couldn't see because it's so dark in here, that's all. But, Auntie, before you go just take a long look at Hedda. Don't you think she's looking nice and voluptuous!

AUNT J: Voluptuous? Oh yes! Yes!

TESMAN: It doesn't show much when she's wearing clothes, true, but I am lucky enough that I see—and feel—

HEDDA: You—feel—nothing!

TESMAN: It was all those cream cakes in the Tyrol, eh? Gobbling away!

HEDDA: I'm exactly the same now as I was when we went away, exactly, precisely—

TESMAN: Don't you agree, Auntie?

AUNT J: All I know is that she is beautiful . . . Hedda is just beautiful.

She takes HEDDA'S *head in both hands, bends it forward, and kisses her hair.*

God bless you, and keep you, Hedda Tesman, for George's sake.

HEDDA: Please . . . don't touch me.

AUNT J: I shall come and see you both every day!

TESMAN: You do that, Julioo.

AUNT J: Goodbye!!

AUNT J. exits.

TESMAN: What are you looking at, Hedda?

HEDDA: Only the leaves. They're so . . . yellow, and withered.

TESMAN: Well, we are in September.

HEDDA: Yes, we are . . . deep . . . into September.

TESMAN: Good old Rina, you know—

HEDDA: Was your aunt offended, Tesman?

TESMAN: What? Oh, that—well, maybe just a little—

HEDDA: But what a vulgar thing to do, to throw her hat down in someone's drawing room, like a kind of scab; it's just not done, Tesman.

TESMAN: No? Well I'm sure she won't do it again, dear.

HEDDA: Anyway, I . . . do want to make it up to her.

TESMAN: Oh, Hedda, that would be so kind of you.

HEDDA: When you go and see them this afternoon, ask her for the evening, how would that be?

TESMAN: She'd be thrilled! Mon amour! You know there's one other thing you could do that would really tickle her.

HEDDA: Yes?

TESMAN: If you could . . . just for fun, you know, just try calling her Auntie Julioo, like I do. I know she'd just love it if—

HEDDA: You are jesting?

TESMAN: It's not that silly—it came about quite naturally, when I was a little boy and I couldn't pronounce "Juliana." It's just that "Miss Tesman" is so—

HEDDA: I shall call her Aunt. That *is* the best I can—do.

TESMAN: Is anything the matter?

HEDDA: It's this room, it needs an upright piano.

TESMAN: What about that one, we could—

HEDDA: No, no. That one—can go to the back. We need another one, right . . .

BERTHE enters.

BERTHE: Pardon me for bargin' in on youse, but that Mrs. Elvsted that brung the flowers before? She's out there and she wants in again.

HEDDA: Mrs. Elvsted? Well take her hat and coat and bring her in, Berthe.

BERTHE exits.

That maid really is such a vulgarian!

HEDDA looks at the card with one of the bouquets.

TESMAN: Mrs. Elvsted . . .

HEDDA: She sent these flowers. I wonder why she's coming here?

TESMAN: Didn't she used to be Miss Rysing?

HEDDA: Yes, Miss Rysing with the repellent hair she was always flouncing about. I was at school with her . . . used to be a flame of yours, didn't she, Tesman.

TESMAN: Till she got tired of me.

HEDDA: *(joking)* Perhaps she's coming to snatch you away!

THEA enters.

Dear Mrs. Elvsted, good morning. How extraordinary to see you after all these years!

THEA: Yes, it has been a very long time.

TESMAN: For me, too! Miss Rysing—er . . . Elvsted—

HEDDA: A thousand thank yous for the pretty flowers. Won't you—

THEA: Oh please. I—I came to see you yesterday afternoon—as soon as I got off the train.

TESMAN: All the way from—haven't you been living way up north somewhere?

THEA: In the country, yes—I—was . . . quite . . . desperate actually . . . when I was told that you weren't at home.

HEDDA: Desperate? Why?

TESMAN: Mrs. Ry—Elvsted, are you—

HEDDA touches THEA's arm.

HEDDA: She's shaking—Mrs. Elvsted. Is something wrong?

THEA: Yes. Yes, there is . . . Oh I'm so sorry to bother you, it's just . . . there is no one else, I—

HEDDA: Here, let's sit down on the sofa.

THEA: No! Please, I'm sorry . . . I can't.

HEDDA: Oh yes you can. Come on now.

TESMAN: Is it bankruptcy, Mrs. Elvsted?

HEDDA: It's something at home, isn't it?

THEA: Yes, well no, I mean . . . Oh God, I—do so want you to understand me.

HEDDA: Then paint the picture clearly, dear.

THEA: Yes. Yes. Well, to start with . . . I should tell you if you don't already know that . . . your old friend, Eilert Lovborg . . . is here in town.

HEDDA: Is he?

TESMAN: Eilert Lovborg, here in town? Well, I see, yes.

THEA: He has been here for eight days in this wild and very decadent city—you know this city is full of temptation for a man like him—I'm so terribly worried—sirens singing everywhere— And, Mr. Tesman, I would so appreciate it if you would, as an old friend, look out for him.

HEDDA: Goodness! But, Mrs. Elvsted, if you don't mind my asking, why are you so distraught about Eilert Lovborg? What has he to do with you?

THEA: Well—he . . . he was the children's tutor.

HEDDA: You have children?

THEA: No, no, my husband's.

TESMAN: Oh, really, well, that's extraordinary. He was . . . uh—balanced enough to . . . hold such a post?

THEA: Mr. Tesman, Eilert Lovborg has been irreproachable for at least two years.

TESMAN: Irreproachable?!

THEA: Perfect, in every way, I promise you, but that was in the country— here in the city, with all the temptations, I'm . . . I'm terrified that he may . . . slip—he may . . .

HEDDA: Become a wild, a dark—thing?

TESMAN: Why didn't he just stay in the north, if things were going so well. Why did he—

THEA: Ohh. Once his book came out he was like a tiger in a cage, he needed—

HEDDA: Air.

TESMAN: Yes! I've heard he has a book—that's wonderful news! What's it . . . uh—

THEA: It's a brilliant book, a history of. . . . Well, civilization, but . . . through a "glass darkly"—that's how I see it . . . it's terribly exciting, you see. It's only been out for two weeks and already it's caused a sensation: he's getting letters, and—

TESMAN: Isn't that wonderful.

HEDDA: Mrs. Elvsted, do you know where Mr. Lovborg is living?

THEA: It took me all day yesterday but I finally got his address.

THEA takes out a piece of paper from her handbag.

I haven't—

HEDDA takes the paper from THEA and gives it to TESMAN.

HEDDA: Tesman, send him . . . an invitation to come and see us this evening. Perhaps we can help him.

TESMAN: What a generous thought, Hedda!

THEA: Oh yes, yes. My husband will be so . . . happy that you . . . are . . . taking care of him.

HEDDA: NOW, Tesman.

TESMAN: Now, you mean this minute?

HEDDA: This minute.

TESMAN: All right, all right, I'll just . . . get my slippers, and . . .

HEDDA: And, Tesman, make it FRIENDLY.

THEA: And—uh—please don't tell him that I asked you, do you mind?

TESMAN: Oh. All right, if you don't want me to!

TESMAN exits to the back room to write the letter.

HEDDA: Well, now we're alone.

THEA: Yes—

HEDDA: Didn't you realize, I wanted to be alone with you?

THEA: I don't know what you—

HEDDA: So that we could talk.

THEA: About what . . .

HEDDA: Mrs. Elvsted, I detest lies.

TESMAN: Lies?

HEDDA: Tell me the truth, please.

THEA: But I have told you the truth, there's nothing more to—

HEDDA: Oh yes there is, there are mouthfuls more. Now come down here and we can have a nice, private conversation.

THEA: No. I'm sorry, I do have to be going.

HEDDA: But you have nowhere to go, do you? Now tell me, dear. How are things at home?

THEA: I'd rather not talk about it, actually.

HEDDA: Oh come on, you can talk to me. After all, we were schoolgirls together!

THEA: Yes, but you were older than me, and . . . and frankly, I was frightened of you.

HEDDA: Frightened? Of me? Really?

THEA: You . . . used to pull my hair . . . whenever you met me alone on the staircase . . .

HEDDA: What? I did that?

THEA: Oh yes, and one day, one day you said you were going to set fire to it.

HEDDA: But surely you know I was just teasing, all schoolgirls—

THEA: Oh I know that now, of course, but then I was young, and—

HEDDA: I remember us as being very close friends. Very. We even used to call each other by our Christian names!

THEA: Oh no! No! I don't think so. We had such different backgrounds, and—

HEDDA: Let's be friends again, shall we? Will you call me Hedda?

She kisses THEA *on the cheek.*

THEA: Oh. You're being so kind to me. I'm . . . I'm not . . . used to it.

HEDDA: And I will call you Thora.

THEA: Thea.

HEDDA: That's what I meant to say. Thea. Thea. Poor Thea, you really aren't used to kindness? Not even in your own home?

THEA: I don't have a home; I've never had one.

HEDDA: From father's home to husband's home. Dungeon to dungeon, hm? Was it like that for you with old Elvsted?

THEA: Oh, Hedda, you can't imagine these past few years—my husband—

THEA shows HEDDA a big bruise on her thigh.

HEDDA: The vicious old bear—

THEA: I was nothing to him, nothing but a useful, cheap—Hedda, my life was truly miserable, and so—I—oh—oh—Hedda, I must tell you my secret or I will faint— The room is spinning.

HEDDA: You can trust me with your soul, Thea.

THEA: Nobody must know, ever, promise me?

HEDDA: I have secrets, Thea, that will go with me to my grave. I am very practised at keeping secrets. Well?

THEA: My . . . husband . . . had no idea I was coming here. He was away and . . . I caught the train and came straight here.

HEDDA: Remarkable. Really?

THEA: What else could I do? What else could I do?

HEDDA: But aren't you afraid of what your husband will do when you go back?

THEA: I'm not going back!

HEDDA: You mean you've left your home forever?

THEA: Yes.

HEDDA: But . . . what will people say?

THEA: They can say what they like!

HEDDA: You are . . . brave, Thea. Heroic! What will you do now?

THEA: I don't know. I only know that if I am to go on living at all, I must . . . be . . . near . . . Eilert Lovborg.

HEDDA: Eilert Lovborg. I see. Tell me, how did this . . . friendship between you and Eilert Lovborg begin?

THEA: Well, as I said, he came to give the children lessons about two years ago.

HEDDA: And the old bear, being a magistrate, was away a lot.

THEA: Yes.

HEDDA: I see.

THEA: It was . . . magic, Hedda! You know, when he first came to us, he was so troubled, dark, and then ever so slowly he began to . . . shimmer, to feel . . . joy again . . . He said . . . that it was all because of me.

HEDDA: What was all because of you?

THEA: That he . . . gave up his sins! Not because I asked him to. I would never do that, but . . . because of his . . . well, adoration, as he put it—

HEDDA: Well, Thea, you must be some kind of angel.

THEA: That's what he says! And in return, Hedda, he showed me—

HEDDA: What?

THEA: How to . . . think. To really think.

HEDDA: How remarkable—

THEA: Hedda, I am a thinker now, every bit as much as any educated man. I helped him with his book—I really helped him; he considers it our book.

HEDDA: Does he?

THEA: . . . we would talk and talk endlessly over—

HEDDA: Your souls—

    HEDDA *makes a hand gesture with* THEA *to say "intertwined."*

THEA: Yes. Oh yes they did.

HEDDA: But, Thea, you don't seem very happy about it.

THEA: But there is . . . something that stands between me and Eilert Lovborg. There is the shadow of another woman.

HEDDA: Oh? Really? Who can that be?

THEA: He said that when they had to part . . . she threatened to shoot him . . . with a loaded gun.

HEDDA: Oh nonsense, people don't do things like that.

THEA: He is . . . haunted by her.

HEDDA: Who is this . . . woman, Thea . . . Who is she?

TESMAN enter with the letter.

TESMAN: Well, here's my epistle, all signed and sealed! Aren't I a good boy?

HEDDA: A very good boy.

TESMAN: Do I get a kiss?

He tries to kiss HEDDA.

HEDDA: Tesman, Mrs. Elvsted is dying to leave. Say goodbye.

TESMAN: Goodbye, Mrs. Elvsted.

HEDDA instructs BERTHE to bring THEA's hat and coat.

HEDDA: Thea, I'll see you to the garden gate.

(to TESMAN) Give it to me before you lose it, Tesman! Tesman!!

HEDDA takes the letter.

BERTHE enters with THEA's hat and gloves and hands them to THEA.

BERTHE: It's the judge, madam; he's right out there.

HEDDA: Judge Brack? Oh. Ahhh— Well? Show him in . . .

BERTHE exits.

(once BERTHE's left) Oh, Berthe!!

BERTHE re-enters.

Put this letter in the post, would you? And no dawdling or gabbing, for heaven's sake!

Judge BRACK enters and BERTHE leaves.

BRACK: *(with a bow)* May one presume to call so early?

HEDDA: Oh yes, of course one may, one may.

TESMAN: You are welcome to our home any time, Judge, any time. Oh! Judge Brack, Miss Rysing.

BRACK: Enchanted.

HEDDA: Judge, how strange to see you by daylight!

BRACK: Am I . . . different?

HEDDA: Much younger.

BRACK: How flattering you are, Mrs. Tesman.

TESMAN: And what about Hedda, eh, Judge? Hasn't she filled out? You know under her nightie she's as fat as a seal!

HEDDA: Tesman, go down on your knees, and thank Judge Brack for his huge generosity!

BRACK: Oh but that was all my privilege!

HEDDA: Dear, sweet judge . . . but look, my friend is panting to leave.

HEDDA takes THEA by the hand.

Au revoir, gentlemen. I shall return in a moment!!

THEA and HEDDA exit.

BRACK: She is looking ravishing, Tesman; is she . . . pleased with . . . everything?

TESMAN: Delirious, Judge, delirious!

BRACK: I'm very glad.

TESMAN: Although she has mentioned some changes she'd like to make, some rather expensive purchases, actually. You know how lavish Hedda's taste is.

BRACK: Yes indeed, Tesman, I wanted to . . . There's something I think I ought to talk to you—

TESMAN: Uh oh, I know, I owe you a mountain of money—

BRACK: Well, don't worry about it just yet, George.

TESMAN: It . . . can't be too long before they'll give me that post—have you . . . you haven't heard anything, have you?

BRACK: Well, only that . . . Eilert Lovborg is back in town.

TESMAN: Yes, yes, and apparently he's pulled himself together—

BRACK: And even written a book!

TESMAN: Yes, I heard about the book.

HEDDA re-enters.

BRACK: We were talking about Eilert Lovborg, Mrs. Tesman.

HEDDA: Oh yes?

TESMAN: I've asked him here tonight, by the way, Judge.

BRACK: Tesman, you ass, you're coming to my place this evening! For my "boys only howl at the moon" party! You promised me last night when I met you at the boat!

HEDDA: Had you forgotten, Tesman?

TESMAN: Completely and totally!

BRACK: Anyway, it doesn't matter, he'll never dare come to this house.

TESMAN: Whyever not?

BRACK: Well, my dear Tesman, and you too, Mrs. Tesman, I have some news that I feel I should share with you.

TESMAN: About Eilert?

BRACK: About you and him.

TESMAN: Well? Please, Judge.

BRACK: It's simply that I don't think you should be well—overconfident about your appointment, Tesman.

TESMAN: What-what-what do you mean?

BRACK: I mean that there may be a contest.

TESMAN: Between me and Eilert? Are you saying Eilert—

BRACK: I have heard that Eilert is now in competition with you for the professorship.

TESMAN: But—but I'm a married man! It was on the strength of the position that we got married. They practically promised me the appointment. We owe hundreds of dollars to everyone; we—

BRACK: Well, you'll have to go through a competition, it's as simple as that.

HEDDA: A dogfight! What fun! Who wants to place bets?

TESMAN: Hedda, how can you joke about this?

HEDDA: I'm not joking, Tesman; I love to watch men fight. It's most erotic, I think.

BRACK: *(after embarrassed pause)* Well, be that as it may, Mrs. Tesman, as your friend and financial advisor, I think that it is my duty to point out to you the situation. And in view of that situation, lavish thoughts or costly purchases would be ill-advised, I'm afraid.

HEDDA: Lavish thoughts, Judge?

BRACK: I'm quite serious, Hedda. Please. Anyway, I'd better be on my way . . . Goodbye. Tesman, when I take my afternoon walk, I'll come and pick you up, all right?

TESMAN: Yes, oh yes, do. Please.

HEDDA: *(lying down)* Judge? I'll only have lavish thoughts about you, I promise! Goodbye!!

> BRACK *exits.*

BERTHE: Goodbye now, Judge; you take care.

HEDDA: Tesman, we really must get a proper butler to show our friends out—that old scrag just won't do. I know you're fond of her but—

TESMAN: HEDDA!!!

HEDDA: Mmmm?

TESMAN: Do you understand what the judge has said?

HEDDA: What, that we are as poor as earthworms after a rain?

TESMAN: Hedda! Listen, with Eilert Lovborg as my rival there's a very good chance I will not get the post! Unless we live very frugally, we may end up on the street.

HEDDA: I thought you were going to take care of me, Tesman.

TESMAN: You knew when you married me I was not a rich man, Hedda; you—

HEDDA: You promised me a salon—where all the great artists and thinkers of Europe would gather—

TESMAN: With my magnificent Hedda at the centre? Oh yes, you should have that, my darling, and you will, one day, I hope, but for right now you'll have to be content sipping tea with me and Julioo and Berty—

HEDDA: I will have my horse? I must have my horse!

TESMAN: HORSE?

HEDDA: Like Velocity, the horse I rode with my father. I have always—had a horse to ride, Tesman.

TESMAN looks away in despair.

I can't have my horse.

HEDDA crosses to her gun cabinet.

TESMAN: I'm sorry to be such a . . . worthless—

HEDDA: No no no no, Tesman, it's all right. I still have one passion left.

TESMAN: You do? Oh, Hedda, I'm so glad, what is it?

HEDDA: My pistols.

TESMAN: Your pistols?

HEDDA: My father's pistols. General Gabler's pistols.

She takes out her father's pistols.

TESMAN: Hedda, please, put those away, for God's sake. Those are dangerous weapons, Hedda! Hedda!

HEDDA laughs and shoots a blank into the air.

End of Act One.

Act Two

Afternoon.

HEDDA is alone downstage left. The sunlight is almost blinding her. She raises her pistol, takes aim, and fires once. We hear the judge, singing, out of sight behind the audience, coming through the back.

HEDDA: Good afternoon, Judge! Back so soon?

BRACK: Hello, Mrs. Tesman!

HEDDA: *(aiming)* I think I'll shoot you, Judge Brack.

BRACK: Put that thing away! For God's sake put it away! This is for creeping in the back way!

She fires.

(closer) Have you gone completely mad?

HEDDA: Awww, poor soldier. Did I hit you? Did I shoot off your hand?

BRACK: Stop these childish games, now!

HEDDA: *(laughing)* Come in, Judge!

Judge BRACK, dressed for a party, enters.

BRACK: Your father would not approve of you playing with his pistols.

HEDDA: Oh no! He was the only one allowed to do that!

BRACK: I must say I fail to see the humour in this really—I mean . . . what were you shooting at?

HEDDA: Just shooting, Judge . . . into the . . . blue!

BRACK: Yes, well, if you don't mind.

HEDDA gives the gun to the judge.

Ah yes, I know this one well.

HEDDA: As do I.

BRACK goes to the gun cabinet.

BRACK: Enough for one day, don't you think?

HEDDA: But now I have nothing . . . to DO, Judge; what EVER shall I DO?

BRACK puts the gun away in the cabinet.

BRACK: Whatever great ladies do: entertain fine friends.

HEDDA: I have no friends.

BRACK: Ha! Tesman not at home?

HEDDA: He trotted off to his aunties'; you're early.

BRACK: Well, yes, if I'd known, I would have come earlier!

HEDDA: But there wouldn't have been a soul here to amuse you, I've been in my room since lunch, changing my clothing.

BRACK: Isn't there . . . a . . . crack . . . perhaps under your bedroom door—

HEDDA: For you to slither in?

BRACK: Through which breathtaking conversation could flow . . . back and forth, as you . . . changed your clothes.

HEDDA: No, Judge, you forgot to arrange for this . . . crack.

BRACK: How stupid of me.

HEDDA: . . . I'm afraid Tesman won't be back for a while. We'll just have to wait, I guess.

BRACK: Oh, that's all right. I'm very patient.

HEDDA: Won't you sit down, Judge?

A short silence.

Well?

BRACK: Well?

HEDDA: I asked first.

BRACK: I have been longing for you to come home, Mrs. Hedda.

HEDDA: Really? So have I. The whole six months.

BRACK: But . . . I thought you were enjoying a most wonderful, passionate honeymoon.

HEDDA: I was unutterably, fantastically bored, Judge Brack. There was not one soul like us to talk to. No one of our calibre, Judge.

BRACK: But . . . but all those beautiful places—the mountains, the—

HEDDA: Every minute of every day with the same person, Judge, the same . . . one . . . man.

BRACK: Morning, noon, and—

HEDDA: Yes. Every minute.

BRACK: I see. But Tesman is a highly intelligent—

HEDDA: Tesman is a monomaniac, Judge; medieval industries in Brabant—

BRACK: Morning, noon—

HEDDA: —and night.

BRACK: But he's the monomaniac you love.

HEDDA: Don't make me vomit!

BRACK: Mrs. Hedda! If you . . . truly feel that way, then . . . why did you—

HEDDA: Why did I marry George Tesman?

BRACK nods.

I had danced myself . . . to a standstill. I was tired, and I needed to rest. You see?

BRACK: No. No I don't.

HEDDA: Anyway, George Tesman is very respectable.

BRACK: Oh, very.

HEDDA: And . . . there's nothing . . . ridiculous about him, is there?

BRACK: No! I—wouldn't say ridiculous!!

HEDDA: The general would have approved, don't you think?

BRACK: Assuredly.

HEDDA: He will always . . . look after me.

Pause.

Judge Brack, I never pinned any hopes on you. You never married, what do you . . . "want"?

BRACK: That's a difficult question.

He stands and crosses to downstage right, facing away from HEDDA.

I suppose a warm and welcoming home that I can wander in and out of—

HEDDA: A sort of friendly "cave"?

BRACK: Where I was regarded as an intimate friend.

HEDDA: By the man of the cave?

BRACK: By the lady. And the man. A sort of . . . happy triangle, gratifying to all concerned . . .

HEDDA: Yes, actually, I often wished for a third person to join us while we were away. God, the two of us, stuck in that railway compartment!

BRACK: Well, it's over now, dear.

HEDDA: It's only just begun. The train has miles and miles and miles to go.

BRACK: Why don't you . . . jump off the train, then?

Pause.

HEDDA: Oh no, no, no. I never jump.

BRACK: Why not?

HEDDA: There are vermin out there, Judge.

BRACK: Waiting—to climb up your legs?

HEDDA: To climb up my legs and—

She makes a "biting" fist.

Oh no, no, no. I'd rather stay where I am. Safe.

BRACK: But what if someone were to join you?

HEDDA: That might be different.

BRACK: An intimate and entertaining friend.

HEDDA: Who would make me laugh, yes. Laugh. That would be a relief.

The front door opens.

BRACK: Ahhh. The triangle is complete.

HEDDA: And the train rushes on.

George TESMAN enters from the hall carrying a number of books.

TESMAN: It's boiling hot out there, look at the sweat, Hedda, pouring down my face! Judge! You're here already!

BRACK: Yes, I came in through the garden.

HEDDA: More books?

TESMAN: A good academic keeps up with everything that's written, Hedda, musn't miss a single word.

HEDDA: Oh no, of course not!

TESMAN: Look! I've bought a copy of Eilert Lovborg's book. I . . . had a . . . look at it on the way home.

BRACK: And?

TESMAN: It's . . . brilliant. He's never written anything like it, I'm afraid . . . Well, I'd better take these into my study and cut the pages before I change for tonight . . . Oh, by the way, Hedda, Auntie can't come and see you tonight.

HEDDA: Oh. It isn't because of the hat, is it?

TESMAN: No, of course it isn't about the hat; how can you think that of Aunt Juliana, Hedda? Auntie Rina is very ill.

HEDDA: Isn't she always?

TESMAN: Today she is much worse. She's having trouble breathing.

HEDDA: Oh. Well then of course her sister should stay with her. I shall have to bury my dismay, that's all.

TESMAN: Yes, you will.

    TESMAN exits.

BRACK: What was that about the hat?

HEDDA: His ugly old auntie put her hat down on the sofa and I pretended to think it was thing's. You know, Berthe's.

BRACK: You naughty girl. Whyever would you do that?

HEDDA: . . . It's . . . the vermin, Judge.

BRACK: The ones that climb your legs?

HEDDA: The very ones . . . they . . . sometimes come . . . sort of . . . screaming out of my mouth without warning, and . . . attack . . . whoever happens to be there.

BRACK: May I suggest rat poison?

HEDDA: But the most frightening thing, Judge, is that preceding the inevitable crushing remorse is a kind of . . . release . . . of exquisite pleasure . . . Isn't that disgusting?

BRACK: But the reason for all this is quite simple, Hedda.

HEDDA: Yes?

BRACK: You are not happy.

HEDDA: And why should I be happy?

BRACK: The house you always wanted?

HEDDA: Ha! I said that once to Tesman—to fill an awkward pause, while we were walking past.

BRACK: But we've made it so . . . comfortable for you!

HEDDA: The rooms smell of lavender and dried roses. Perhaps Julioo—

HEDDA takes a flower from a vase.

—brought that with her.

BRACK: More likely it's the lingering scent of the late owner, the illustrious Mrs. Falk.

HEDDA: Yes, there is something of a death rattle about it. Oh, Judge, I am going to be bored.

BRACK: Then you must find . . . a passion, a calling!

HEDDA: Political power, what do you think? Be the éminence grise behind George Tesman?

BRACK: Tesman?

HEDDA: Doesn't have the stuff?

BRACK: Or the money.

HEDDA: Or the money.

BRACK: Hedda. Hedda, what you need is a . . . transforming experience!

HEDDA: Yes!

BRACK: And that will undoubtedly come within a year or so, don't you think?

HEDDA: That will NEVER come. NEVER, NO!

BRACK: Never?

HEDDA: I have no gift for it. I am not like . . . other women, don't you understand?

BRACK: Oh—

BRACK takes HEDDA's head in his hands.

—but you are.

HEDDA: There's only one thing I have a gift for—

BRACK: And what is that?

HEDDA: Boring myself to death. Now you know. Ahhh. Here comes Tesman "the professor."

TESMAN comes in, dressed for the party.

TESMAN: Hedda, has any message come from Eilert?

HEDDA: No.

TESMAN: Then he'll be here any minute, I bet.

BRACK: Do you really think he's going to come?

TESMAN: Oh yes, if we're going to compete I know he'll want to compete as friends, as comrades! After all, we've been quite happily competing for years.

BRACK: I'll invite him to my party, shall I?

HEDDA: And if he doesn't want to go, he can stay here with me.

TESMAN: But, Hedda dear . . . would that be—

HEDDA: You forget, Mrs. Elvsted is coming! The three of us will have a nice, quiet—

BRACK: Cup of tea, ha, that's about all Eilert Lovborg *(crosses to upstage left)* can handle, isn't it?

HEDDA: Eilert? I daresay he's stronger than you think.

BERTHE appears. TESMAN is wild-eyed.

BERTHE: Ma'am? There's some kind of gentleman here to see you . . .

HEDDA: Well show him in, Berthe!

TESMAN: He's here. I knew it! I knew it!

Eilert LOVBORG enters from the hall.

Eilert!

TESMAN shakes LOVBORG's hand.

How nice to see you again after all these years!

LOVBORG: Thanks for your letter, George. I appreciate it. May I shake hands with you as well, Mrs. Tesman?

HEDDA: We're very glad to see you, Mr. Lovborg.

Pause.

I don't know if you two—

LOVBORG: Judge Brack, isn't it?

BRACK: It's been some time.

TESMAN: Eilert, I want you to think of this as your home, isn't that right, Hedda? I . . . hear you're planning to settle in town again, is that right?

LOVBORG: I'd like to.

TESMAN: That's nice! Oh! By the way, I managed to get a hold of your new book! I haven't really had a chance to read it yet, but—

LOVBORG: Oh . . . I wouldn't bother with it.

TESMAN: Why not?

LOVBORG: Because it isn't much good.

BRACK: But it's been so well received.

LOVBORG: Of course! Because I wrote the rubbish I know everyone wants.

BRACK: Very sensible.

TESMAN: But, Eilert, why would you—

LOVBORG: Well, I had to re-establish myself, didn't I, to open people's minds to my work again.

TESMAN: Ohhh! Yes, I see.

LOVBORG pulls out a manuscript.

LOVBORG: This is my real book. THIS you can read, George Tesman—it I have written with my blood.

TESMAN: Oh. Really. I see . . . what what . . . is IT about then.

LOVBORG: The future, Tesman.

TESMAN: The future? But how can you say anything about the future?

LOVBORG: There is something to be said about it. Here, have a look.

TESMAN: But this is a beautiful hand, Eilert; when did YOU—

LOVBORG: I dictated it—a wonderful luxury . . . See, it's in two parts. The first deals with the invisible dark forces present today . . . that will inevitably shape our future, and the second is a close look at the future—as I see it—

BRACK: And how is that?

LOVBORG: Oh . . . a sort of highly impressive but . . . grossly misshapen monster, Judge Brack.

BRACK: Hm.

TESMAN: Amazing. I would never dare—

HEDDA: No, you wouldn't.

LOVBORG: I brought *it* with me because I hoped to read some of it to you this evening.

TESMAN: Oh! Well I'd love it, but—

BRACK: I'm giving a party tonight, Mr. Lovborg, in honour of Tesman, really—

LOVBORG: Oh, well then, another time!

BRACK: Won't you do me the honour of joining us?

LOVBORG: No. Thank you very much.

BRACK: Please, Mr. Lovborg, there'll only be a few of us. It will be great fun, very lively, as Hed—um . . . Mrs. Tesman always says.

LOVBORG: Oh, I am sure that *it* will. All the same—

BRACK: I know! You could bring your manuscript along and read it to Tesman at my place! I could lend you a room!!

TESMAN: That's a fine idea! What do you say, Eilert?

HEDDA: Tesman, Mr. Lovborg doesn't WANT to go. I'm sure Mr. Lovborg would much rather stay here and have supper with me.

LOVBORG: With you, Mrs. Tesman?

HEDDA: AND . . . Mrs. Elvsted.

LOVBORG: Oh, yes, I ran into her for a few minutes this afternoon.

HEDDA: You did? Well she's coming here this evening, Mr. Lovborg, so you really must stay. Otherwise she'll have no one to see her home!

LOVBORG: Oh. I see. Well, all right, thank you very much, Mrs. Tesman—I will stay.

HEDDA: Good. I'll just go and tell Berthe.

She goes over to the gun cabinet and rings a handbell. BERTHE enters. HEDDA takes BERTHE to a back room, discusses the snack, and sends BERTHE to the kitchen.

TESMAN: Um . . . uh . . . Eilert . . .

TESMAN bumps LOVBORG and the manuscript falls; he then picks it up.

Oh pardon me.

LOVBORG sits in a chair.

I just wanted to ask you, is it . . . the future—that . . . uh . . . you're going to . . . lecture on?

LOVBORG: Yes it is.

TESMAN: They told me down at the bookshop that you're going to hold a series of lectures here during the autumn.

LOVBORG: Yes, I am. I hope you don't mind—

TESMAN: No, of course not, my God, it's just . . . well . . . this is so embarrassing.

LOVBORG: George, you're afraid my lectures might harm your chances . . . for the professorship?

TESMAN: No no, forget it, I can't expect you to put them off for my sake—

BERTHE enters from the back room with a tray of punch and biscuits.

LOVBORG: Listen, George. I'll postpone them until you've been given your appointment. How's that.

TESMAN: WHAT? I thought you were competing with me—

LOVBORG: George, I'm not interested in being a professor. Not at any price. I found that out while I was in the country.

BRACK: What ARE you interested in then, Lovborg?

LOVBORG: Honour! And at the risk of sounding too solemn—making a real and lasting contribution.

BRACK: Yes, well, with a past like yours, I suppose—

TESMAN: Honour! Hooray!! Auntie Julioo was right after all. Honour! Oh I knew it, I knew it. Hear that, Hedda? Eilert is NOT going to stand in our way!!!

HEDDA: OUR way?

TESMAN: What about you, Judge Brack? What do you think about all this, eh?

BRACK: Honour? I think it's rubbish, of course.

TESMAN: Do you, Judge? Really?

HEDDA: Tesman, you look as if you've been struck by a thunderbolt.

TESMAN is in some kind of emotional hysteria signifying relief.

TESMAN: Yes, I feel like that! Exactly! A thunderbolt!

HEDDA: Gentlemen!! Won't you go in and have a glass of cold punch?

BRACK: One for the road? Eh? Yes, why not?

TESMAN: Brilliant idea, Hedda, just brilliant. Oh. I don't think I've ever felt so happy. Truly!

HEDDA: Mr. . . . . Lovborg? Will you—

LOVBORG: No! No, thank you very much.

BRACK: Good Lord, there's nothing poisonous about a glass of cold punch, man!

LOVBORG: Not for you.

HEDDA: Never mind. I'll take care of Mr. Lovborg.

TESMAN: Oh yes, Hedda dear, would you?

TESMAN kisses her.

As they go off upstage right into the back room we hear TESMAN say:

Marvellous hostess, my wife—a real aristocrat—

HEDDA finds a photo album.

HEDDA: Would you . . . like to see some . . . photographs?

LOVBORG stands.

Tesman and—

TESMAN looks into the front room.

—I passed . . . through the Tyrol on our way—

She sits on the sofa, and LOVBORG moves to the sofa and sits.

. . . home . . . This uh . . . mountain range here, right here, Mr. Lovborg, it's . . . the Ortler Range. Tesman has written the name underneath, do you see? "The Ortler Group near Meran."

LOVBORG: Hedda . . . Gabler!!!!

HEDDA: No!

LOVBORG: Hedda . . . Gabler!!!

HEDDA: That . . . was . . . my name . . . once.

LOVBORG: So from now on for the rest of my life I must learn to stop saying HEDDA GABLER.

HEDDA: Yes, you must stop, you must stop now.

LOVBORG: Hedda Gabler married? To George Tesman?

HEDDA: So . . . the world goes—

LOVBORG: Oh Hedda, Hedda, how could you bury yourself alive?

HEDDA: Stop it.

Judge BRACK *peers at them.*

Stop it.

LOVBORG: Stop what, Hedda?

TESMAN enters.

HEDDA: And this, Mr. Lovborg, is taken from the d'Ampezzo Valley. Just . . . look at those rock formations . . . What's the name of that . . . peculiar range, dear?

TESMAN: Let—

TESMAN sits on the sofa.

—me have a look . . . oh yes, those are the Dolomites, of course.

HEDDA: Ohh yes, those are the Dolomites, Mr. Lovborg.

TESMAN: Hedda, I was just wondering if you'd like a glass of punch?

HEDDA: Yes, I will, thanks. And . . . a few biscuits.

TESMAN: Cigarettes?

HEDDA: No!

TESMAN: Olé! Punch and bickies coming up!

He goes back. BRACK *sits in the back room and glances from time to time at* HEDDA *and* LOVBORG.

LOVBORG: How could you do it, Hedda? How could you?

HEDDA: If you go on calling me Hedda, I won't be able to talk to you!

LOVBORG: Can I not call you Hedda when we're alone?

HEDDA: No! You can think it, but you mustn't say it.

LOVBORG: Because of your love for George Tesman?

HEDDA: Love? Don't be ridiculous.

LOVBORG: You don't love *him*?

HEDDA: I will never betray him.

LOVBORG: Hedda, just tell me one thing.

HEDDA: Shhh.

TESMAN enters from the back room with a tray.

TESMAN: Here you are! Goodies!

He puts the tray down on the sofa table.

HEDDA: What are you doing, Tesman? Why didn't you get Berthe to bring it in?

TESMAN: Because I love to serve you! Is that all right?

HEDDA: But you've filled both glasses, Mr. Lovborg—

TESMAN: But Mrs. Elvsted will be here soon, won't she?

HEDDA: Oh yes! She will!

TESMAN: Had you forgotten her?

HEDDA: Well we've been so . . . engrossed . . . in these . . . Do you remember this little village?

TESMAN: Oh yes, it's the one at the bottom of the Brenner Pass. Where we spent the night—

HEDDA: And met all those lively summer visitors.

TESMAN: Yes, that's right. I only wish we'd had you with us, Eilert. Yes.

TESMAN kisses HEDDA's cheek.

He goes into the back room and sits down with BRACK again.

LOVBORG: Will you just tell me one thing?

HEDDA stares at him.

Was there no love in your feeling for me?

HEDDA turns away.

I know there was. You thrum with it still!

HEDDA: We had . . . most stimulating conversations, we were good friends; you were very—well, frank.

LOVBORG: At your command! You wanted to know every detail of everything? Why?

HEDDA: Do you find it so incredible that a young girl should want a glimpse into the world forbidden to her?

LOVBORG: So you only wanted knowledge from me? Hedda, there was something more—say it, say it!

HEDDA: Something exquisite that no one else has ever dreamed or imagined.

LOVBORG: Yes, yes. There was, there was. Hedda, remember those afternoons when the words fell out of our mouths so fast and, and—

HEDDA: —filled the room with small tornados?

LOVBORG: *(laughing)* Yes, yes! With your father the great general snoring in the next room—

HEDDA: Dreaming of battlefields!

LOVBORG: I told you all my secrets, secrets so entombed in my soul I didn't know they were there? You—you listened to my secrets, even to my days and nights of . . . insane depravity, Hedda! What power did you have that I poured myself out—

HEDDA: Power? I . . . had power over you?

LOVBORG: You always will, Hedda Gabler . . . I know that you loved me; why else would you have heard my sins—

HEDDA: They were my sins too, Eilert, to hear them was to breathe!

LOVBORG: Why, why did you send me away, Hedda Gabler?

Judge BRACK looks back.

HEDDA: Have you forgotten your . . . violation of my absolute trust in you, the last time we were alone?

LOVBORG: You should have killed me. Why didn't you shoot me?

HEDDA: My fingers would not move; they were paralyzed with FEAR.

LOVBORG: Of?

HEDDA: Talk. Scandal.

LOVBORG: Coward!

HEDDA: Oh yes. I have always been a coward. Not like your Thea. Your Thea is a brave girl.

BRACK looks into the front room.

LOVBORG: Thea is nothing.

HEDDA: Nothing?

LOVBORG: To us.

HEDDA: And I am a coward. Luckily for you. Come here, Eilert, I want to tell you a secret.

LOVBORG: Yes?

HEDDA: My not killing you was not . . . my most cowardly failure . . . that evening . . .

LOVBORG: Oh, Hedda! Hedda Gabler!

He embraces HEDDA from behind—a sexual moment—then HEDDA breaks away.

As the embrace ends:

HEDDA: I can't! No. I can't.

She gets a mirror from a desk drawer and checks her lipstick. BERTHE enters with a candelabra.

BERTHE: She's back again, madam, that Mrs. Elfstar with the angel's hair.

HEDDA sets the candelabra on the desk.

HEDDA: Thank you, Berthe. Please show her in, show her in.

BERTHE turns and exits. LOVBORG pauses. THEA enters.

HEDDA greets THEA graciously.

At last, Thea dear, I am so glad you've returned.

THEA nods at LOVBORG, who sits on a chair by the sofa.

THEA: Should I—say hello to . . . Mr. Tesman, or—

HEDDA: No, darling, leave them alone, they're going out anyway.

THEA: Going out?

HEDDA: To howl at the moon, and drink bathtubs of wine.

THEA: Oh.

(to LOVBORG) You're not going, are you?

LOVBORG: No, *(crosses to sit on sofa)* Thea, I am not.

HEDDA: Mr. Lovborg is staying here with us.

TESMAN lights candles.

THEA: Oh! Ohhh good. You can't imagine how happy I am . . . to be here.

HEDDA: No, Thea!! Not there. Come over—

She "helps" THEA move to the chair.

—here and sit beside me. I want to be . . . in the middle.

HEDDA sits on the sofa.

THEA: As you wish.

LOVBORG: *(after a pause)* Isn't she lovely to look at?

HEDDA: Only to look at?

LOVBORG: Oh yes! We're like brother and sister, aren't we, Thea? We trust each other implicitly.

THEA: Hedda, he says I've inspired him!

HEDDA: How gratifying for you.

LOVBORG: She's courageous, too. Like a lion.

THEA: Me? Courageous?

LOVBORG: It takes a good deal of courage to leave the respectability of home, of—

HEDDA: Dungeon more like. Didn't you know that, Eilert, about old Elvsted?

LOVBORG: It still took courage.

HEDDA: Yes. If only I had some.

LOVBORG: Yes?

HEDDA: Then life *would* be worth living.

LOVBORG: Yes.

HEDDA: Thea, dear, will you have a nice glass of cold punch?

THEA: Oh! No thank you, I never drink anything like that.

HEDDA: Mr. Lovborg?

LOVBORG: No thank you, Mrs. Tesman. I don't either.

THEA: He doesn't either.

HEDDA: But I want you to, Eilert.

LOVBORG: No, thank you.

HEDDA: You lied. I have no power over you.

LOVBORG: Not where this is concerned.

HEDDA: But *it* is crucial that you have a drink, Eilert.

THEA: Hedda!

LOVBORG: Why?

HEDDA: Because people will think you are weak!

THEA: Oh, Hedda, no!

LOVBORG: People can think what they like!

THEA: Exactly.

HEDDA: I saw it so clearly, blindingly, in Judge Brack when you were too timid to join them in there.

LOVBORG: Timid? I wanted to stay here with you!

THEA: There's nothing timid about that, Hedda.

HEDDA: I even saw the judge winking at Tesman when you were too frightened to go to his party!

LOVBORG: Do YOU think I'm timid, Hedda, is that what you think?

HEDDA: That's what Judge Brack thought.

LOVBORG: Well let him.

HEDDA: So you're not going, then?

LOVBORG: No. I'm NOT. I'm staying here, with you and Thea.

THEA: Of course he is, Hedda.

HEDDA: God you are a strong man—the strongest? That's what I told Thea when she came in this morning weeping and trembling, fearing that just because you were in the city you were . . . revelling with prostitutes and . . . eating live rats and such—

LOVBORG: What?

THEA: Hedda!

HEDDA: So there's no need for any more trembling, Thea. You see, he's all right.

LOVBORG: What is happening, Mrs. Tesman?

THEA: Hedda, what are you—

HEDDA: Shhh, that odious Judge Brack is watching.

HEDDA waves at BRACK.

LOVBORG: Revelling with prostitutes.

THEA: Hedda! Why are you doing this?

LOVBORG: You swore your trust! You swore it on your life.

THEA: Eilert, darling, please listen to me!

LOVBORG: Skol, Thea!! To treachery.

He empties a glass and takes another.

THEA: Hedda! Why would you want this to happen?

HEDDA: Want what to happen, Thea?

LOVBORG: And here's to you, Mrs. Tesman, for telling the truth.

He drinks.

Are you proud of yourself? Tracking me down, like some kind of criminal? Such cold self-righteousness. Now you tell the truth. Did your husband send you? Did he *miss* me at his card table?

THEA steps towards LOVBORG.

Stay away from me!

TESMAN and BRACK enter.

BRACK: Well, Mrs. Tesman—

HEDDA: Time to go, gentlemen?

LOVBORG: Time for me too, Judge Brack.

THEA: Eilert, please don't.

HEDDA: *(pinching her)* Stop whining.

THEA: Ow!

HEDDA crosses to downstage left.

LOVBORG: As you were kind enough to ask me.

BRACK: You're coming then?

LOVBORG: If I may.

BRACK: Delighted.

LOVBORG: *(to TESMAN)* Tesman! Listen. There are one or two things I'd like to show you before I . . . hand it in to the printer.

The back room candles are blown out.

TESMAN: Oh, well, I'm honoured, Eilert.

THEA: Eilert.

LOVBORG: Thea, please forgive my ungenerous words. I lost control.

THEA: Eilert, don't go.

LOVBORG: I will go and I will show you and the world that I am standing strong and I will not fall again.

TESMAN: Uh oh, Hedda, how are we going to get Mrs. Elvsted home?

HEDDA: Mrs. Elvsted?

LOVBORG: I will come for you about ten o'clock—is that all right, Mrs. Tesman?

HEDDA: I think that sounds wonderful.

TESMAN: Don't expect me home at ten o'clock, Hedda!

HEDDA: My dear, you can stay as long as you like.

THEA: So . . . I'll wait for you here, shall I . . . Mr. Lovborg?

LOVBORG: Yes.

BRACK: Well, gentlemen, on to the great bacchanal!! Good night, ladies.

HEDDA: Indeed.

They exit and BERTHE *has finished blowing out the candles and has exited.* HEDDA *follows and* THEA *steps to look out the window.*

THEA: Oh, Hedda, Hedda, what will happen now?

HEDDA: At ten o'clock he'll be here, on fire, singing, with vine leaves in his hair.

THEA: What are you talking about, Hedda Gabler? What do you mean?

HEDDA: I mean a human being cannot live in fear . . . of himself!

THEA: I think that's nonsense.

HEDDA: YOU can doubt him as much as you like, Thea; I have unshakable FAITH.

THEA: Why are you doing this, Hedda? When you know how this will turn out? What's the true reason?

HEDDA: The true reason? I want to hold a human destiny. In my hands. I want to have some—

THEA: Oh, Hedda, you mean . . . you want to . . . play a part, be an inspiration, as I was?

HEDDA laughs.

But surely you have—a husband—

HEDDA: Who wants power over worms? You don't understand, Thea, how . . . poor I am—a beggar—and you . . . so . . . glittering . . . rich.

HEDDA touches THEA's hair.

I think I will burn your hair off after all!!

THEA: Let go, let me go!!!

THEA pulls away.

You're scaring me, Hedda!

BERTHE enters.

BERTHE: Your supper's ready in the dining room, madam. I got a roasted chicken with oranges; I got a pile of baked potatoes, with nice butter melting all over 'em; I got garden tomatoes—

HEDDA: Marvellous, Berthe. A thousand thanks for your hard work. We'll be there in just a moment.

BERTHE withdraws, suspiciously.

THEA: No. No, I'm going to go home, alone, in the dark. Right now.

THEA starts to leave.

HEDDA: You're going to stay here and eat your dinner, little rodent. And then at ten o'clock Eilert Lovborg will arrive, shimmering with vine leaves in his hair.

HEDDA guides THEA to the back room to have dinner.

End of Act Two.

Act Three

THEA is reclining, wrapped in a shawl, in an armchair near the stove, and HEDDA is asleep on the sofa, fully dressed with a blanket over her. She is dreaming.

THEA dreams, wakens, stands, and looks at HEDDA.

THEA: Oh God oh God oh God!

BERTHE enters with a letter, startling THEA terribly.

Are they here, are they here?

BERTHE: I'll tell ya when they're here, Mrs. Elvsted.

THEA: But who was—

BERTHE: Just a shiverin' girl with a letter, that's—

THEA: A letter! Oh, give it to me, it must be—

BERTHE: It's not for you, it's for the doctor. It's for the doctor and nobody else.

THEA: I'm sorry. Please forgive me, I—

BERTHE: It's from his auntie, Miss Juliana Tesman, and it's only for Georgie.

BERTHE puts the letter on the desk.

I'll just set it here on the table. I'm sure it will be safe here.

THEA: Yes, of course.

BERTHE: Oh, Jesus in heaven those candles are burned right down all over. I'll just . . .

THEA: Yes, I imagine it will soon be light.

BERTHE: It is light, madam.

> *BERTHE gathers up THEA's blanket.*

> *THEA opens sheers and dawn light pours in.*

THEA: Ohhh God, God, dawn already, and he's still not back.

> *BERTHE checks the stove.*

BERTHE: Well, whatja expect, for mercy's sake?

THEA: What do you mean?

BERTHE: I MEAN, that when I heard that Mr. Loverboy there had come back to town and then I seen him go off "to drinkin'" with the boys there, I seen the devil a-lickin' his lips.

THEA: I beg your pardon?

BERTHE: Well everyone know about Eilert Lovborg, madam; every person in this town has some story. Mercy, my cousin Sophie—

THEA: Be quiet, for heaven's sake, you'll wake your mistress.

BERTHE: God know she needs her sleep now, eh? Eh? Here, do you want a bit more on the fire?

THEA: No, thank you, I'm quite warm.

BERTHE: I never seen someone shiver when they're warm but if that's what-cha want!

HEDDA wakes up when BERTHE exits.

HEDDA: Who's that?

THEA: Just your . . . maid . . .

HEDDA: What am I doing here? What time is it?

THEA: After seven I think.

HEDDA: When did Tesman get back?

THEA: He hasn't.

HEDDA: Really?

THEA: No one has.

HEDDA: And we were waiting for them till—what—four o'clock!

THEA: All night!

HEDDA: We should have saved ourselves the trouble.

THEA: Did you manage to sleep?

HEDDA: Yes, actually, I think I slept fairly well. Didn't you?

THEA: No. I couldn't, Hedda; how could I?

HEDDA: Now, now, there's nothing to worry about. I know exactly what happened—

THEA: What? Please tell me.

HEDDA: Well . . . obviously their party went on very late—

THEA: Yes, but—

HEDDA: And knowing Tesman, he didn't want to come home and wake us all up in the middle of the night.

THEA: Where would he have slept?

HEDDA: At his aunties' of course.

THEA: No. There was a—

THEA takes the letter to HEDDA on the sofa.

—letter from them this morning.

HEDDA: Really?

HEDDA looks at the letter in THEA's hand.

Oh yes, that's "Julioo's" handwriting. Well he must have stayed at the judge's then. And Eilert Lovborg is sitting there with . . . maybe . . . weeds in his hair, reading aloud.

THEA: Very funny.

HEDDA: Brainless little pest.

THEA: All right.

HEDDA: You look tired to death.

THEA: Yes, I am tired to death.

HEDDA: Go to my room and lie down for a little.

THEA: Oh no—

HEDDA: Don't argue with me, do what I say!

THEA: But I couldn't possibly sleep.

HEDDA: Of course you can. Go on.

THEA: All right, *(crosses to the back of the theatre)* but I want to know as soon as—

HEDDA: I'll tell you when your beloved arrives.

THEA exits. HEDDA opens a second sheer.

HEDDA goes to the gun cabinet, rings the bell, then goes to the desk and gets hairpins from on top. BERTHE enters.

BERTHE: You called?

HEDDA: For heaven's sake, put some more wood on the stove, I'm freezing!

BERTHE goes to the wood pile in the back room and carries wood back to the stove.

BERTHE: I know! It's practically snowin' in here!

HEDDA: Well do something!

BERTHE: Yes, yes I will. Madam.

BERTHE opens the stove.

As BERTHE adds a log to the fire:

The room'll be warm in the clap of a hand. The CLAP of a—

A door slams.

Ahh! Thank the Lord in heaven, I think it's them!

HEDDA: Well go and show them in. Hurry, Berthe.

She gives her blanket to BERTHE.

I'll look after the fire!

BERTHE: Don't burn yourself now!

HEDDA tends the fire, putting wood in. TESMAN enters and tiptoes across the backroom

HEDDA: Good morning!

TESMAN: Hedda! Good God what are you doing up?

HEDDA: Shhhh! Mrs. Elvsted is sleeping in my room.

TESMAN: Mrs. Elvsted? Do you mean . . . she stayed the night?

HEDDA: No one came for her.

TESMAN: No, hm I suppose not.

HEDDA: Did you have a ripping time?

TESMAN: Yes, well, fascinating and illuminating. Especially at the beginning when Eilert read his book to me.

HEDDA: And?

TESMAN: It's one of the most remarkable books ever written, Hedda, it—it will change . . . the way people think. It could . . . change the course of history . . . it's really . . . that . . . original.

HEDDA: I know it is.

TESMAN: Hedda, Hedda, I felt the most awful . . . evil . . . well, base jealousy, when he'd finished reading, I . . . honestly didn't think I had it *in* me, it's been tearing me up ever since—have you ever felt . . . anything like it?

HEDDA: No. I can't say I have.

TESMAN: And what's even more shameful is the kind of savage joy I feel . . . in knowledge that he's irredeemable.

HEDDA: Don't you mean courageous?

TESMAN: Ha! I don't think you would have called him courageous last night! Hooo!

HEDDA: Why, what happened?

TESMAN: Well, let's just say the polite party quickly turned into a rather bacchanalian orgy, Hedda. Really I'd never seen anything like it—these men that I know . . . doing the most . . . vulgar, horrendous—and your handsome Mr. Lovborg . . .

HEDDA: Did he have vine leaves in his hair?

TESMAN: Vine leaves? Oh no, we were indoors, Hedda. It, it— It was just as Auntie always says, he was like a werewolf, from the fairy tales, he went from man to . . . monster. It was appalling but before he did he stood up and delivered the most . . . heartfelt panegyric to the woman who had inspired this . . . great work. Oh! He was weeping and . . .

HEDDA: Did . . . he name her?

TESMAN: No, but it was clearly Mrs. Elvsted—he talked about her golden hair and—

TESMAN weeps.

HEDDA: Whatever *(crosses to sofa)* are you crying about. Tesman!

TESMAN: But it's not really my fault, I was trying to help . . .

HEDDA: Spit it out, Tesman.

TESMAN: He's the one who dropped it—they were all drunk as stevedores, worse. And, and I fell behind at one point, in order to . . . vomit . . . I wasn't well at all, and there it, there it was, you see. I decided not to give it to him because of the state he was in—

HEDDA: WHAT, Tesman?

TESMAN: His . . . manuscript! His priceless, perfect . . . on the road!

He pulls it out of his cape.

HEDDA: I see . . . did you tell the others?

TESMAN: No! No! I didn't want to . . . humiliate him.

HEDDA: So nobody knows that you have Eilert Lovborg's manuscript.

TESMAN: Not a living soul.

HEDDA: And he didn't ask about it?

TESMAN: He vanished. And then a few of us went back to the fellow with the bits of red hair's place . . . for morning coffee and . . . oh dear, I think I'd better lie down before I run it back to his place—

He swoons onto the sofa.

HEDDA: TESMAN! Get up this second and go to bed!

TESMAN: Oh no, no, I'd better run over right now and give it to Eilert—I'll wake him up and—

HEDDA: No. Let me read it first.

TESMAN: Read it? You never read anything I write, Hedda.

HEDDA: Just . . . give it to me.

TESMAN: But, but, there's no copy of it, he told me—this is the only one!

HEDDA kisses and hugs TESMAN.

HEDDA: You toddle off to bed, dear, while I read it, all right?

TESMAN: But if he should miss it, Hedda—he'll be desperate!

HEDDA: Oh!

HEDDA picks up the letter.

I forgot, Tesman, there's a letter for you.

TESMAN: A letter!

He takes the letter from HEDDA and puts the manuscript on the table.

Perhaps—

He opens the letter.

It's from . . . oh God . . . *(weeping)* Oh no . . . Auntie Rina is dying . . .

HEDDA: Well, Tesman, we have been expecting it.

TESMAN: It says if I want to see her again I must rush . . . oh God, God . . . I'll run up there right now.

HEDDA: Run?

TESMAN: Oh, Hedda, would you . . . come with me?

HEDDA: Oh no, Tesman, no. I can't bear sickness or dying. You must never ask me—

TESMAN: Oh God, I hope I won't be too late, I hope I won't be too late.

HEDDA: You won't be too late, Tesman, if you rushhhhhh. JUST in time to see her eyes . . .

BERTHE enters.

BERTHE: Georgie? The judge man is here, wanting to socialize. I told him this is a terrible time.

TESMAN: Impossible, oh yes—

HEDDA: It's a most propitious time for me, dear Berthe. Show Judge Brack in, please.

BERTHE exits.

Tesman, the manuscript!

Both TESMAN and HEDDA go for the manuscript.

He tries to get it but she takes it back—he is so upset about Rina he gives up. As HEDDA puts the manuscript in a desk drawer, BRACK enters.

Tweet tweet tweet, early bird!

BRACK: I am, yes.

(to TESMAN*)* What's wrong with you?

TESMAN: My aunt Rina is dying. I'm just—

BRACK: Oh, Lord, well don't let me—

TESMAN: Berthe! Berthe!

> TESMAN *goes off to find* BERTHE *and they leave together. Pause.*

HEDDA: Well, Judge, I hear you had a wild party—an orgiastic party—last night.

BRACK: Hedda, there is something I must talk to you—

HEDDA: Has . . . something happened?

BRACK: Eilert Lovborg erupted like a kind of mad volcano all over the streets and I've come to tell you beware!

HEDDA: Slow down, Judge, please, tell me, what happened?

BRACK: Well, it started at my place, this . . . alarming transmogrification . . . he became more and more frenzied—

HEDDA: Spewing hot lava at all of your startled faces?

BRACK: Hedda! This is very serious, listen. After he left my place he stormed . . . a house of . . .

HEDDA: A WHOREhouse, Judge?

BRACK: Yes! yes! And after having his fill, he turned into a kind of fiend, breaking all the windows, calling them all dirty thieves, ripping the curtains— And then, Hedda, he attacked two police officers so savagely he almost killed them. It took a half a dozen strong men to drag Eilert Lovborg to jail.

Pause.

HEDDA: So . . . No vine leaves after all?

BRACK: Vine leaves? You haven't fallen for that, have you? Hedda, the man is a ruthless . . . and he will use you—

HEDDA: Use me, Judge Brack?

BRACK: Use your kindness, your attachment—your home. He will cause a scandal—no one else will have him, every respectable house will be closed to him! He'll use your house as a refuge, to meet and . . . stroke that woman—his mistress, here in this house.

HEDDA: What are you saying, Judge?

BRACK: You must close your doors to Eilert Lovborg—I will not have him here.

HEDDA: What?

BRACK: He . . . he's an intruder, Hedda; he brings disgrace. I'd not want him here. I have no . . . home when he is here and . . .

HEDDA: You want to be the only cock . . . of the walk . . . Is that it?

BRACK: Yes, yes I do, Hedda. And I will fight for that right . . . to the death.

HEDDA: You are a . . . dangerous man, aren't you?

BRACK: I am?

HEDDA: Thank God you have no power. Over me.

BRACK: No?

HEDDA: Thank God you're just a . . . what do you call those castrated cocks? Oh yes, capons.

BRACK: Most humorous, Hedda. I know you will think about what I said. We must avoid scandal . . .

HEDDA: Going out through the back way, Judge?

BRACK: Yes, I have nothing against back ways. Sometimes they can be most . . . mysterious and enthralling, Mrs. Hedda.

HEDDA: Even when pistols are fired—

BRACK: Do people shoot their tame cockerel?

HEDDA: I don't know, do they?

> *BRACK exits. HEDDA makes sure that she is alone, then goes to the desk, retrieves LOVBORG's parcel, and is about to look at it when LOVBORG enters.*

Mr. Eilert Lovborg. We've been waiting for you all night.

LOVBORG: Forgive me.

HEDDA: You've come for Thea.

LOVBORG: Would you please—

HEDDA: How do you know your little Thea is still here?

LOVBORG: They told me at her lodgings that she'd been out all night.

HEDDA: You went to her lodgings . . .

LOVBORG: Is . . . Tesman up yet?

HEDDA: No, no he isn't.

LOVBORG: Did he . . . say anything to you?

HEDDA: Just . . . that he had a rather wild time.

LOVBORG: Is that all.

> LOVBORG *sits on the sofa.*

HEDDA: Yes, that's all—Eilert . . .

> LOVBORG *drops in despair.* THEA *appears.*

THEA: Oh, Eilert, finally! Are you . . . all right?

LOVBORG: Thea. It's . . . all over.

THEA: What do you mean.

LOVBORG: I mean it's all over for me.

THEA: No, no. Eilert, don't say that.

LOVBORG: You'll say it yourself when you hear what—

THEA: Don't tell me, I don't want to know, it doesn't matter—

HEDDA: Perhaps you two would rather be alone?

LOVBORG: No, Hedda, I want you to stay, please.

THEA: I don't want to hear anything, Eilert!

LOVBORG: Thea, listen to me. You mustn't, you can't be part of my life.

THEA: What?

HEDDA: I knew it!

LOVBORG: I have no *(stands)* further use for you, Thea, I'm sorry.

THEA: No further use? How can you say that to me, after—listen to me, Eilert, we will forget all this and we will go back to work—

LOVBORG: I'm giving up the work.

THEA: No! You are not! I'm not going to let you give up because of one bad night; our book—

LOVBORG: OUR book. Yes it is.

THEA: Our book is going to come out, and everyone will honour and respect you again—I want to share—your joy—

LOVBORG: Thea, our book will never come out.

HEDDA: Ahhh.

THEA: What do you mean?

LOVBORG: What I said; don't ask me any more.

THEA: Eilert, what are you talking about? Has anything happened to our book?

LOVBORG: Don't ask me that, Thea, please.

THEA: Eilert, I want to know; I have a right to know.

LOVBORG: *(spontaneous rage)* I've destroyed it. I tore it in a thousand pieces.

THEA: No, no it's not possible.

LOVBORG: I've destroyed my life, why not my life's work?

THEA: You did that last night? You tore—

LOVBORG: Yes, into a thousand pieces, which I then scattered into the fjord. A long way out. In the cool salt water, so they can drift, with the current and the wind, and then . . . sink, deeper and deeper, just like me, Thea.

THEA: *(screaming) No!!!!!*

> *THEA attacks him.*

No!

LOVBORG: Yes!

THEA: You . . . it's like killing a little child.

LOVBORG: I know.

HEDDA: A child.

THEA: How could you kill my child? How could you? How could you?

> *She sobs on the floor, then gets up.*

You're right, Eilert, it is all over. Goodbye, Hedda.

HEDDA: Where are you going?

THEA: I don't know. There's nothing but darkness ahead of me now.

THEA exits.

HEDDA leans against the edge of the window.

HEDDA: Aren't you going to see her home, Mr. Lovborg?

LOVBORG: Me? Through the streets? What would people think?

HEDDA laughs.

HEDDA: Is it really so awful? What you did last night?

LOVBORG: Oh, last night was only the beginning, Hedda. I can feel it, rampaging through me. I have no strength against it now. She has loosed it with her doubt.

HEDDA: Thea has sent you back to your wild, your dark life—

LOVBORG: I can't even go back to that now. No. Her loss of faith has—

HEDDA: That little fool was trying to shape a man's destiny! Even so, I don't know how you could be so very savage with her.

LOVBORG: Don't say I was savage, don't say that.

HEDDA: To tear apart something more precious to her than her own life. Don't you think that was savage?

LOVBORG: I can tell you the truth, Hedda. I didn't destroy it.

HEDDA: Oh? Then . . . where is it?

LOVBORG: To kill a child isn't the worst thing a father could do.

HEDDA: I know *that*.

LOVBORG: What would be even worse . . . to forget it. To lose *it*.

HEDDA: You lost your masterpiece?

LOVBORG: Yes! I lost it, like a glove! Isn't that ridiculous?

Hysteria.

HEDDA: Eilert! It is only words after all!

LOVBORG: It *is* Thea's pure soul. And I—have—Hedda, this beast inside me has the power of Hell, and I am nothing, a slave. I have to end it—I must end it.

Pause.

HEDDA: Yes, you must—free yourself, Eilert. You must—free yourself. And do it . . . beautifully.

LOVBORG: Beautifully?

He laughs.

With vine leaves in my hair?

HEDDA: Oh no, I don't believe in vine leaves anymore. But I do believe in—you.

She kisses him.

Beautifully, Eilert. Go.

LOVBORG stands.

LOVBORG: Goodbye, Mrs. Tesman. Remember me to your husband.

HEDDA: Wait.

She stands, crosses to the gun cabinet.

I want to give you . . . something to remind you of me. A keepsake.

She takes out a pistol case, goes to the desk, opens the case, removes the pistol, and goes to LOVBORG.

You recognize it? You looked in its mouth once.

LOVBORG: You should have used it then.

HEDDA: Take it. Use *it* now.

HEDDA puts the gun in LOVBORG's hand.

LOVBORG holds the pistol.

LOVBORG: Thank you.

HEDDA: And beautifully, Eilert Lovborg, promise me!

LOVBORG: Goodbye, Hedda Gabler!

He exits upstage left. HEDDA goes to the desk, removes the manuscript, opens the stove, lights a match and holds it to a candle, and then lights a page of the manuscript, putting the page in the stove, then slowly crumples the rest of the manuscript and adds it to the fire in the stove.

HEDDA: I'm burning your child, Thea. Lovely Thea, with the golden wavy hair. The child Eilert Lovborg gave you. I'm burning it. I'm burning your child.

End of Act Three.

Act Four

Evening. The drawing room is in darkness. HEDDA, *dressed in mourning, is playing a Chopin nocturne on the piano.* AUNT J, *in mourning dress, including black hat and veil, enters from the hall.* HEDDA *finishes the piece, turns, sees* AUNT J, *and goes to her, holding out her hand.*

AUNT J: She passed over, Hedda; I swear, I saw her soul sucked up through her head, and then she just . . .

A gesture of collapse.

HEDDA: I know, Miss Tesman, as you can see. Tesman sent me a . . . card . . . I'm sorry.

AUNT J: I told Georgie, I said, "I want to go tell her myself; two women talking . . . quiet about death, in this . . . grand house of life—"

HEDDA: That was very kind of you.

AUNT J: Rina wanted me to tell you she's sorry! She whispered to me: "This is not time for Hedda's house to be in mourning!" She knew, you see.

HEDDA: Did she die peacefully?

AUNT J: Ohhhh yes, ever so. You should have seen her, Hedda! Berthe and Georgie and I all had our arms wrapped around her and our faces this close, and just like a baby, going to sleep— Has . . . Georgie not come back yet, dear?

HEDDA: No. He said in his card not to expect him for a while. Can I offer you something warm?

AUNT J: Ohhh no thank you, dear, I don't dare! I have to run back and dress Rina, in her favourite dark green, and I have to lay her out, you know, with her hands crossing over her heart? And her hair just . . . she's my sister and I want her to go to her grave looking . . . perfect.

HEDDA: Is there anything I can do to help?

AUNT J: Oh, Hedda, you don't want your hands touching death at a special time like this, or even your thoughts!

HEDDA: I have no power over my thoughts, Miss Tesman.

AUNT J: Oh yes you do, Hedda, yes you do. Ahh! Look at the dark, I must get home right away and start sewing Rina's shroud . . . I hope I'll be doing some sewing here, before long, dear, and I don't mean a shroud!!!

TESMAN enters.

TESMAN: Auntie Julioo!

TESMAN kisses AUNT J.

I . . . did most of the things you asked, I think; it's just . . . my head is spinning, and . . .

AUNT J: Georgie dear, you mustn't take it so hard!

TESMAN: What? Oh, *well*—

AUNT J: She's free now, George, of all that pain! Those—claws she cried about so much!

TESMAN: Yes, yes, I know, Auntie, I—

HEDDA: Will you be lonely now, Miss Tesman?

AUNT J: Ohh! Rina's room won't stay empty for long.

TESMAN: What? Who are you going to—

AUNT J: There's always some poor invalid person wants special care needing to be spoon-fed, to be turned over in bed so they won't get the bed sores.

HEDDA shudders—an awkward pause.

And anyhow, I have a delicious feeling there'll be precious work to keep me busy over here, soon! Praise God.

HEDDA: Oh please.

TESMAN: Oh yes, Auntie, we'll have a wonderful time when *that* happens.

HEDDA groans, quietly.

AUNT J: Well, I must be getting home to Rina now. Good heavens. I've just had the strangest thought, Hedda. Rina is in heaven with Georgie's father, my brother, and on earth with me at the very same time!

TESMAN: On earth and in heaven!

AUNT J: Goodbye!

She exits.

HEDDA: What have you heard? Have you heard anything about Eilert?

TESMAN: Well, I ran over to tell him his manuscript was safe, but he wasn't there; I was frantic and then I met Mrs. Elvsted in the street and she told me that he'd been here this morning and that he told her he'd torn his manuscript to shred! Is that true?

HEDDA: That's what he said.

TESMAN: Did you . . . tell him we had it?

HEDDA: No. Did you tell Thea?

TESMAN: No, I . . . didn't. But why didn't you tell Eilert we had it, Hedda? He must be desperate about it, suppose he were to do himself harm? Give it to me, I'll run it over right now. Now, Hedda.

HEDDA: I haven't got it.

TESMAN: What do you mean you haven't got it?

HEDDA: I burnt it. The whole masterpiece.

TESMAN: You burned Eilert Lovborg's book? You BURNED—

HEDDA: Don't shout like that, thingy will hear you.

TESMAN: BURNT it? I can't believe my ears. You didn't, you didn't!

HEDDA: Oh yes I did.

TESMAN: Do you realize what you've done? It's a criminal act, it's disposal of lost property! HEDDA! How could you do such a monstrous thing? ANSWER ME!!!! ANSWER ME!!

He throws HEDDA to the ground.

HEDDA: *(on the floor)* I did it for you, George.

TESMAN: What? What are you talking about?

HEDDA: When you came home this morning? And you were talking about how threatened you'd felt . . . by . . . this book . . . I couldn't stand it. I couldn't stand for that book to . . . hurt you. So—

HEDDA cries.

TESMAN: *(as she cries)* Are you telling me the truth? You are, aren't you? Oh God. Hedda, I'm sorry.

He embraces her.

I'm sorry! Oh you do love me, I see that you do, in your eyes, you know . . . I'll confess, this is the first time I've ever truly . . . felt it—

HEDDA: George. George, I have a secret I want to tell you . . .

He leans forward, ready.

No, you'd better go and ask Auntie Julioo. She seems to know all about it.

TESMAN: Noooo! REALLY? Really? Hedda!!!!!

HEDDA: Shhhh! Thing will hear you!

TESMAN: Who? Oh, you mean Berthe? My old Berty? Well let's tell her now, she'd love to know!

HEDDA: *(a sound of desperation)* I can't breathe, George; I'm sick; I can't breathe.

TESMAN: Oh, dear—

He helps her to the sofa. HEDDA sits.

—must be your condition, here I'll open the—

HEDDA: They don't open wide enough, George, you know that!

TESMAN: There, there, it's all right, just . . . calm down, calm down. Don't worry, I won't tell Berthe anything.

HEDDA: It's all right, tell her if you want.

TESMAN: No. No, she can wait. But if you don't mind, I would like to tell Auntie Julioo, it might cheer her up in this dark—Hedda? Do you know what makes me happiest of all? You finally called me George! I bet you didn't even know—

HEDDA: George.

They kiss.

TESMAN: Oh, Auntie J will be very very happy.

He lays his head in her lap.

HEDDA: Will she be happy that I burnt Eilert Lovborg's masterpiece for you?

TESMAN: Oh no, we won't tell anyone that—no, Hedda. THAT will be our secret.

(touching her) OH, Hedda, the . . . fierceness of your love; I had no idea that women—

HEDDA: Love ferociously?

TESMAN: Oh God, Hedda, I am . . . fearful for *Eilert*!!

THEA enters, wearing her hat and coat, with a bag of manuscript notes.

THEA: Oh, Hedda, forgive me for coming back—

HEDDA: What's happened, has something happened?

TESMAN: Has something happened to Eilert?

THEA: I—think he may have had some kind of accident!

HEDDA: Why? Why do you think that?

THEA: Because . . . because I heard them talking about him at my boarding house, when I went in, the most terrible rumours, all around town—

TESMAN: Yes, yes, I've been hearing them too!!

HEDDA: What—

HEDDA steps downstage of the sofa.

—were they saying at the boarding house?

THEA: They stopped talking as soon as they saw me.

TESMAN: Perhaps you misunderstood them, Mrs. Elvsted.

THEA: No.

THEA steps downstage.

Oh no, I didn't . . . I heard them say something about a hospital.

TESMAN: Hospital!

HEDDA: That's impossible.

THEA: That had me so frightened I went to *his* lodgings and I asked to see him . . . they . . . they said he hadn't been back there since yesterday afternoon!

TESMAN: Yesterday afternoon?

THEA: Something terrible has happened, I know it!

TESMAN: Hedda, why don't I go into town and . . .

HEDDA: Stay out of it!

Judge BRACK *enters.*

TESMAN: Judge! Hello! What—what—

BRACK: I thought I should let everyone know that Eilert Lovborg has been taken to hospital. He's dying.

THEA: Oh God, oh God!!

TESMAN: Dying?

HEDDA: Oh.

THEA: OH, Hedda, Hedda, we . . . parted as enemies.

HEDDA: Hush, Thea!

THEA: I must go to him! I must see him before he dies!

BRACK: No.

BRACK stops THEA.

Mrs. Elvsted . . . No one's allowed to see him now.

THEA: But what's happened to him! TELL me, what's happened—to him?

TESMAN: He didn't . . . uh . . . did he?

HEDDA: Of course he did.

TESMAN: Hedda!

BRACK: I am afraid you are right, Mrs. Tesman.

THEA: Oh no, no!

TESMAN: Suicide! God!

HEDDA: SHOT himself!

BRACK: Right again, Mrs. Tesman.

THEA: When . . . did this—

BRACK: This afternoon, between three and four.

TESMAN: Where—was he when—

BRACK: I'm not . . . sure of that . . . I only know . . . that . . . he'd shot himself in the chest—

THEA: To think of him dying like that!

HEDDA: In the chest, Judge Brack?

BRACK: Yes.

HEDDA: Not . . . in the temple?

BRACK: In the chest, Mrs. Tesman.

HEDDA: In the heart . . . yes, yes, that's good too.

BRACK: Whatever do you mean?

HEDDA: Nothing, I don't mean anything.

TESMAN: And . . . the wound is—

BRACK: It is a mortal wound. He's very probably dead—now.

THEA: Yes, he is. I can feel it. He is . . . dead . . . oh, Hedda!

HEDDA: Thank God! Thank God!

TESMAN: Hedda, what are you saying?

HEDDA: I'm saying . . . that there is . . . great beauty in what he has done.

BRACK: MRS. TESMAN!

TESMAN: Beauty! What an astonishing thing to say, Hedda!

THEA: How can you talk about beauty? Eilert is dead, *dead*! Don't you understand that?

HEDDA: Eilert Lovborg had the courage to do what he had to do.

THEA: Nonsense, he was tortured—mad!

TESMAN: He was a desperate, poor man.

HEDDA: No he wasn't!

THEA: He was— He, he tore up our book! He—

BRACK: Do you mean that manuscript of his? He tore that up?

THEA: Yes, last night, he told me so!

TESMAN: Oh, Hedda, we're never going to escape this, never!

BRACK: That's very strange.

TESMAN: It's . . . it's, it's horrifying to think of him . . . dying . . . without leaving behind . . . that . . . book . . . It would have made him immortal—it—it—

THEA: Oh yes, yes, if only it could be pieced together again!

TESMAN: Oh I would give my life to—

THEA: Well, you know, it might . . . be possible.

TESMAN: What?

THEA: I-I—have kept . . . his notes for the book!

HEDDA: Ahh.

TESMAN: You have the notes?

THEA: Yes! Yes—

She crosses to sit on the sofa and then opens the folder.

—here they are, see? I brought them with me when I left home and—and—

TESMAN: May I . . . ?

THEA: They're not in any order; they're completely mixed up—

TESMAN: Can you imagine, if we could work it out? Perhaps—perhaps if we helped each other.

THEA: Oh yes! Yes!

TESMAN: We will, I'm sure we can. I'll devote my life to it.

HEDDA: Your life, George?

TESMAN: Well, all the time I can spare. My own book will have to wait. This is far more important, Hedda, and I owe it—to Eilert's memory.

HEDDA: Perhaps.

TESMAN: Well, Mrs. Elvsted, let's . . . just . . . pull ourselves together if we can—after all, there's no sense in crying over something that's happened, that we can't un . . . do . . .

THEA: Oh yes, Mr. Tesman, I know, I know!

TESMAN: Good. Good. Let's have a look at these notes right away. Hm. Where shall we sit, here? No, let's go in the back room. Would you excuse me, Judge?

BRACK: Please go ahead.

TESMAN: Come with me, Mrs. Elvsted!

THEA: Oh God. Please let this be possible!!

TESMAN lights a lamp on the piano. TESMAN and THEA go into the rear room. They sit at the piano and absorb themselves.

HEDDA leans against the wall.

HEDDA: Oh, Judge . . . there is such . . . release . . . in what Eilert Lovborg has done.

BRACK: Release? Well, release for him, I suppose, in a way.

HEDDA: Release for me!! To know that someone has been BRAVE, truly . . . godlike and beautifully brave!

BRACK: Hedda, listen to me!

HEDDA laughs.

HEDDA: You boring old mole! Get away from me.

BRACK: Eilert Lovborg meant a great deal to you, didn't he?

HEDDA: I'm not going to answer that. Eilert Lovborg is a hero. He lived his life the way he wanted to, till—*vivre libre ou mourir*, Judge.

BRACK: I'm sorry to shatter your glassy illusions, but he did not shoot himself. Not the way you think.

HEDDA: What are you talking about?

BRACK: In the first place, he's already dead.

HEDDA: I know that!

BRACK: And it happened in a house of whores!

HEDDA: Liar.

BRACK: Yes, Mrs. Hedda, he was there this afternoon caterwauling about thieves and weeping some incomprehensible story about a lost child . . .

HEDDA: He was found in a whorehouse?

BRACK: YES, Mrs. Hedda! With a discharged pistol in his breast pocket. And a mortal wound.

HEDDA: In the heart.

BRACK: No, it was not in the heart, my dear girl, it was actually . . . somewhat lower . . . if you take my meaning . . . rather appropriate for—

HEDDA: Everything I touch becomes vile and ludicrous!

BRACK: Another thing, Hedda.

HEDDA: Yes?

BRACK: The pistol . . . he had with him . . .

HEDDA: What about it?

BRACK: It was stolen!

HEDDA: Stolen! Oh no, that's not true!

BRACK: But . . . It must have been stolen—

TESMAN appears from the back room as THEA blows out the lamp.

TESMAN: Listen, Hedda, it's almost impossible for us to see anything under that lamp.

HEDDA: Yes?

TESMAN: Would you mind if we use your writing table?

HEDDA: All right, all right. No! Wait a minute, let me clear it first.

TESMAN: No, no, you don't need to do that, there's—

HEDDA: I said let me clear it. I'll just . . . put these things on the piano for now.

She puts papers and a gun on the piano.

Here.

TESMAN sets a chair at the desk and helps THEA set her chair; they sit.

Dear Thea . . . and how is it going with Eilert Lovborg's resurrection?

As BERTHE enters with candelabra.

THEA: Well, it's going to be very difficult.

TESMAN: But we've got to do it; we must; we *will*—after all, it is what I'm best at . . . sorting other people's papers . . . luckily—for Eilert!

HEDDA has trouble breathing.

HEDDA: What were you saying about the pistol?

BRACK: That he must have stolen it.

HEDDA: Why do you think that?

BRACK: Because any other explanation is unthinkable, Mrs. Hedda.

HEDDA: I see.

BRACK: Eilert Lovborg was here this morning, wasn't he?

HEDDA: Yes.

BRACK: Were you alone with him?

HEDDA: For a few moments.

BRACK: You didn't leave the room while he was here?

HEDDA: No.

BRACK: Have you checked to see if both pistols are there?

HEDDA: No.

BRACK: Well, don't bother. I saw the pistol Lovborg had when they found him. I recognized it right away.

HEDDA: Have you got it.

BRACK: Oh no. The police have it.

HEDDA: And . . . what will the police do with it?

BRACK: Well, try to trace the owner.

HEDDA: Do you think . . . they'll succeed?

BRACK: No, Hedda Gabler.

He touches her hair.

As long as I am quiet.

HEDDA: And if you talk?

BRACK: You could always say he'd stolen it.

HEDDA: I'd rather die.

BRACK: *(laughing)* Little Hedda. People say things like that. But they never actually do them.

HEDDA: And suppose the pistol wasn't stolen? And they find the owner? What then?

BRACK: Then there will be a scandal, Hedda— Everybody will talk.

HEDDA: A scandal?

BRACK: Why did you give Eilert Lovborg the pistol, Hedda? What will people say when they learn?

HEDDA: I didn't think of all this.

BRACK: Well, as long as I keep quiet about it—

He touches HEDDA's *waist.*

—there's no danger.

HEDDA: So I am in your power, Judge?

BRACK: Hedda, dear, I will not abuse my position.

He fondles HEDDA's *left breast.*

HEDDA: I am a slave, once more.

She struggles to breathe, in obvious distress.

BRACK: Oh come on, most people can resign themselves to the inevitable, sooner or later.

HEDDA: Is that what most people do? George? How is . . . the work coming? Will it—be all right?

TESMAN: Oh God knows, Hedda, there's months of work here, months and months—

HEDDA: It's heroic what you're doing? Don't you find it strange, Thea, sitting here with Tesman, as you used to sit with Eilert Lovborg?

THEA: Oh, if only I could inspire your husband in the same way!

HEDDA: I'm sure that you will, in time.

TESMAN: Oh yes! Yes, I can feel it even now, it's quite extraordinary! Listen, Hedda, why don't you go and sit down with the judge. I'm sure you two—

HEDDA: Is there nothing I can do? To be of USE? Nothing?

TESMAN: Oh heavens no, Hedda. Judge? You don't mind entertaining our Hedda for a while, do you?

BRACK: Not at all—it would be my greatest pleasure!!

HEDDA: How kind, Judge, but . . . I'm very tired . . . I think I'll just go back and lie down, if . . . nobody minds . . .

BRACK reads a magazine.

TESMAN: Oh! Yes, dear, do!

HEDDA goes to the back room. She sits at the piano. As her fingers touch keys, HEDDA plays a frenzied dance tune. THEA is shocked.

Hedda! Please, darling, if you don't mind, dance music seems . . . rather inappropriate! Think of Auntie Rina! And Eilert!

HEDDA: And Auntie—Julioo-oo-oo!

TESMAN returns to the desk, sits.

Don't worry, from now on I'll be very quiet!

HEDDA snuffs the candles then looks at TESMAN and THEA.

TESMAN: Poor Hedda, I think it really distresses her to see us doing this morbid work. She's quite sensitive, I think. WAIT. I have an idea! Mrs. Elvsted, why don't you move in with my auntie Juliana! Then I could come up in the evenings, and we could sit and work there!

THEA: Oh! Well, yes, I'd be—

HEDDA: I can hear what you're saying, Tesman!! How do you think I'm going to spend MY evenings?

TESMAN: Oh I'm sure Judge Brack will be kind enough to come over and see you! You won't mind if I'm not here, will you, Judge?

BRACK: I'll come every evening, Mrs. Tesman. We'll have a . . . most enthralling time together.

HEDDA: You'll love that—

She removes her jacket and reaches for the gun.

—won't you, Judge? The only cock on the dungheap!!

. . . cock on the dungheap.

HEDDA aims the gun at her head. She shoots herself. She falls to her chair.

BERTHE enters. TESMAN and THEA stand. THEA picks up the candelabra from the desk.

TESMAN: Oh she's playing with those pistols again!

He runs to the back room.

Oh my God, she's shot herself! in the . . .

BRACK throws his magazine to the floor.

BRACK: Oh no. No. Good God. People don't do things like that!

Black.

Actors exit in blackness.

Sirens: Elektra in Bosnia

Sirens: Elektra in Bosnia was first produced by Peggy Shannon and Ryerson University for the Women in War Project in Hydra, Greece, from July 3 to 5, 2012, with the following cast and creative team:

Agamemnon: Stathis Grapsas
Boy: Felix Beauchamp
Cassandra: Kaleigh Gorka
Clytemnestra: Cynthia Ashperger
Elektra: Kira Guloien
Goran: Ayinde Blak
Iphigenia: Rebecca Liddiard
Laza: Andrew Pimento
Menelaus: Matt K. Miller
Orestes: Tal Shulman
Servant and Camera Woman: Madeline Smith
Soldiers: Andrew Lawrie, Andrew Robinson, Jordan Campbell
Chorus: Aliyah El-Amin, Angela Dodson, Annabel Harvey, Carina Oliveira, Caryn Chappell, Courtney Muir, Maria-Clair MacIsaac, Meaghan Silva, Rhanda Jones, Samantha Varona, Sierra Chin Sawdy, Madeline Smith, Sophia Thompson-Campbell, and Vicky Houser

Director and Producer: Peggy Shannon
Production Stage Manager: AJ Laflamme
Composer: Jake Vanderham
Choreographer: Alyssa Pires

Characters

Agamemnon
Boy
Cassandra
Clytemnestra
Elektra
Furies
Goran
Iphigenia
Laza
Melor
Menelaus
Orestes
Prisoner
Soldier

Prologue

The three FURIES enter:

FURIES: We / are the / FURIES / the furies / the furies
The feared
The flaming
Ferocious
The furies
We SOAR through the sky
Yes we fly
Through the years
Ten thousand years
Over wars
Under lives
In between
Man and wife
Mother and child
Sister and brother
Sister and sister

And we see
What we see
And when we see
One of ours

Mother
Daughter
Woman

Slaaaaain
Slauuuughtered
Des-e-crated

Three rough breaths.

Oh we froth at the mouth
And we fly we catch we TIE
Him up in poioioioioisonous
SNAKES
To the stake
Of his conscience / conscience / conscience
Oh we flame
Oh we fire
Oh we burn
Him to ashes / ashes / ashes
Just WATCH US
Beware / beware
We are here for all mothers
For all daughters
We avenge
We pursue
We will never give up
Till we have YOU!

(as they retreat) Beware . . .

Scene One

The woods. A man sets up an execution. Two other men stand around, joking. They are Goran (G), Laza (L), and Melor (M).

M leads ELEKTRA on stage and seats her facing the action; he adjusts her face so she can look carefully.

FURIES: *(whispered)* Elektra . . .

L walks with his cellphone.

G: Laza, it's freezing out here, man.

L: We gotta wait for General Menelaus to get back.

G: Hey, man. I gotta get home for dinner, what's keeping him?

L: Why, what are you having for dinner?

G: Roast chicken, baked potatoes, and apple pie with homemade ice cream. JEALOUS?

L: YEAH. It's just me and my brother. Pizza every night.

G: No matter how many bombs we have, we always have pizza. Come on, Laza, my hands are freezing. Lemme just shoot the poor bastards and get it over with. There's only five hundred of them . . . They're cold too, death'd be better than this cold; we'd be doin' them a favour.

L: We can't go ahead till he gives us the word.

G: He's going to give us the word; he always gives us the word. Let's just go ahead . . .

M: Are you crazy? You want to be court-martialled? And if there's any younger than fourteen again . . .

G: There's NOBODY younger than fourteen—are you kidding? We aren't animals like them.

M: That photo was all over the news, man, with you shooting the kid? All over CNN and BBC.

G: He didn't LOOK like a kid!

L: You were so high on crystal meth you didn't know what he looked like!

M: That BBC Nigel guy, films the whole operation and we're ALL so high we don't even—

G: How the hell did you let a JOURNALIST . . .

L: He didn't tell us he was a journalist—he said he was a soldier, wanted to be part of the operation. He spoke perfect Serbian. A lot of guys won't do this one, too much blood.

M: ANYWAY, because of that, we gotta hold BACK. It's delicate now. No more mistakes.

PRISONER: Please, sir, can you give this boy some water?

L: Look at that kid, he's just a boy.

G: He's sixteen if he's a day!

L: His uncle told us he was only thirteen. You heard him. You pretended not to.

G: SHUT UP. I gotta get home.

L: Your wife on your case?

G: You could say that.

M: Mine is always asking me, what are you doing? What are you DOING with those boys, walking them into the woods? What happens in the woods?

L: Setting up camp. That's what you tell them, setting up camp.

G: Mine says I smell like blood. She won't let me touch her . . .

M: Oh Jesus look at that . . . Pissed himself.

PRISONER: Please, he is so frightened; he is just a boy, won't you—

G: Shut up.

M: That's what I'm talkin' about. He's not EVEN fourteen.

L: My son is fourteen. This kinda gets to me, I have to say.

G: This is war, ladies. They're the enemy. Are you forgetting what they have done to US? I saw my neighbour's baby flying through the air; I saw my girlfriend hanging from a tree . . .

L: I'm just saying. We could . . . just . . . you know, let the kid go. He might even be like twelve. Look at him shaking, come on.

G: Okay, Laza, just to appease you. I'll make a special deal with him.

L: A deal?

M: Don't do anything irregular, man, or we'll be next.

G: Kid. Hey, kid, come here.

PRISONER: Take me, please. Not the boy.

G: It's okay, it's okay, man, we're not gonna hurt him. Just wanna talk to him.

PRISONER: It's okay. Go.

G: Boy. What's your name?

BOY: Yasmine.

G: Yasmine, nice name. I grew up with a Yasmine. How old are you?

BOY: . . . What?

L: How old are you?

BOY: Um . . . thirteen.

G: That's what I was telling them!

M: Told you! TOLD you!

G: Shut up. You look smart. I bet you're good at math.

BOY: I am, first in my class. I can help you, I can . . . calculate . . . distances, and and firepower and—

M: You remind me of my nephew—big talker—you'll go far, if you have the chance.

L: We have to let him go, Commander said. NATO is watching, no one under sixteen.

G: I'll tell you what. We got your women just over the hill, in a kind of holiday camp—you know that, right? We don't kill women; only YOUR guys do that. We never hurt a woman. Only a little fun now and then. Now I heard that your mother is over there, isn't that right?

The BOY turns back to his uncle, who nods.

So the guys and I, we, you know, we have huge hearts, we're pussycats—we like to let you fellas go if we can, so we thought of a game.

BOY: A game?

G: If you call your mother—

BOY: Call my mother?

G: Just with your voice. Just stand here, and call for her as loud as you can.

L: What the hell?

G: Call and call, and if she answers, if we see her up on the crest of the hill there, you go free. You both go free, you, your mom, and even your uncle there.

What do you think?

The BOY looks back at his uncle, who does not trust them at all.

M: We're not messing with you, kid, I promise.

L: Promise on my own son.

G: We just want to give you the chance—

M: To call . . .

G: For your life. Are you in?

The BOY *nods.*

BOY: I have a very loud voice. I will win this game!

M: Okay, kid, it's now or never.

L: Just her name. Over and over, as long as it takes.

The BOY *slowly walks to a designated spot, takes a deep breath, and calls.*

BOY: REEEEMAAAA. REEEMAAAAAA. REEEEMA. REEMAAAAAAAAAAA.

He uses every cell of energy in his being and collapses to his knees.

L: Look. I think I see her. Look at that, on the hill!

G: Holy shit.

M: We gotta keep our word, man.

G: Of course we keep our word! I am a man of my word.

L: Kid—you're free. Go on . . . go to your mother.

PRISONER: You must tell your men over the hill to let them go, or they will kill them both.

G: Shut up.

M: He's right. Bratislav loves to shoot that gun of his. Don't worry, man, I'll give the commander a call.

He does.

Bratislav?

M murmurs into his phone.

L: What do you think, little man? You're free. Go give your mother a big kiss.

M: They will be safe.

M guides the kid.

Yasmine. Go. Go to your mother.

BOY looks in shock, walks very shakily away, falls once, gets up, keeps walking.

L: Uncle. You go too.

PRISONER looks shocked.

Yeah. We promised. WE keep our word!

G: That's good. I feel good about that. You feel good about that, Melor?

M: He was under fourteen. It's the law.

L: I wish the BBC coulda seen THAT.

G: Anyway, we got the rest of them to take care of. Let's get on with it. General Menelaus is gonna give us the word—to shoot. He always does. And when he finds out what we done today? We'll get humanitarian awards. So, Laza, go tell the poor suckers it's time to pray!

L: *(yelling)* Men and boys of Srebrenica, this is your last minute, your last minute to smell the grass, hear the wind, feel the ground under your knees, your tongues in your mouths, to hear your own voices . . . Speak! Speak to your ALLAH.

A cellphone rings.

(answers) . . . yes, General. Right away.

M: He wants us to go ahead?

L: I gotta tell you. I was sorta hoping we wouldn't have to kill today.

G: Why? Are you goin' soft on us?

L: No, man. We're running low on bullets, and so many of 'em we have to shoot twice because you are such a lousy shot!

G: Hey! I'm a hell of a lot better than you! You don't even know how to HOLD a gun . . .

L turns away, nods at G, who is smoking. They all position their guns. Shoots. Shoots Shoots. Pauses.

Looking forward to that roast chicken and gravy. Oh man, I can taste it now!

They exit, laughing . . .

Scene Two

ELEKTRA steps forward.

ELEKTRA: I was three years old, and I was on a ship with my mother and my father. We were standing on the deck together, looking at the sea when it was just turning to night; it was warm and windy and I was snuggled between the two of them, and the three of us, so close together, looking out at the swirling blue-grey ocean, was maybe the best and safest feeling I ever had. And then my mother, my beautiful mother, whispered in my ear that she had a secret she wanted to tell me. I was very excited as I thought that maybe the secret was the dappled white horse I had so been longing for, but no, no! She leaned into me and whispered with her hot sweet breath that I was going to have a baby sister.

And we were going to name her Iphigenia.

She then offered me a sip of her cherry juice; she lifted the glass to my mouth and I remember biting down as hard as I could on that glass, and shattering it. My mouth was full of warm blood and glass and I just kept trying to chew the glass—my mother was screaming and the world was turning, but my father was calm, his voice like a blanket he said, "Spit, my little princess, just keep spitting out that glass until there is no more."

I think of that moment often, the moment before the secret, the three of us, on that ship, and for a second I am in that bliss, but then, very quickly, it fades: my father is not there, my mother is not there. I am alone.

I am all alone on that boat—my mother is in the water, screaming for help; my father dead at my feet; the boat is burning.

And I am the cause
I am the cause

And that is why
I am here
That is why the FURIES plucked me from my hiding place and
Brought me here
Because I will tell you a secret—

FURIES: *(one at a time)* SECRET, SECRET, SECRET

ELEKTRA: This is Hell

FURIES: *(one at a time, overlapping)* HELL, HELL, HELL

ELEKTRA: I am burning

FURIES: *(intoning)* BURNING

ELEKTRA: In Hell
Because of who I am
Because I am Elektra

FURIES: *(shriek, overlapping)* ELEKTRA, *ELEKTRA*, *ELEKTRA*

ELEKTRA: Because I killed my mother

FURIES: Yes!

ELEKTRA: I murdered

The FURIES breathe three fast breaths.

My mother
The woman who gave me life
I can't believe it

I can't comprehend it
I used to hide under her skirts
To wait for her all day at the window
To sing with her in church
To brush her hair for hours
I am in Hell and I put myself here
I killed my own mother with these hands
Did you see that massacre?
Five hundred innocent people
Shot dead
It happens every day here
YES this is my Hell
The *FURIES* have decreed it
They have a special Hell for those who kill their mothers

FURIES: SSSSSSSSS

ELEKTRA: And for my sinful hatred of my sister

FURY ONE: SINFUL HATRED OF MY SISTER

ELEKTRA: I am to suffer like my sister

FURIES TWO & THREE: SISTER, SISTER

ELEKTRA: To watch a massacre
As she did
And then be tortured

FURY ONE: TORTURED

ELEKTRA: To death
As she was
Every day
For eternity
FOREVER

FURIES: FOREVER, FOREVER, FOREVER

ELEKTRA: Unless
Unless!
I am somehow . . . redeemed

FURIES: REDEEMED

ELEKTRA: Yes!
There is a possibility of some kind of . . . salvation here
Of mercy!
And that is why you are here!
The furies say I can only be redeemed
By you
By your mercy
And you will only know if I deserve mercy
By hearing my story!
Will you listen to my story?
Will you be my witness?
I can still see her face
Her fear
Her eyes imploring
Her last words were:
"I love you, my girl"

FURIES: *(one, two, then three)* I LOVE YOU, I LOVE YOU, MY GIRL

ELEKTRA: He was my father
And she . . . was my mother
And OH I miss him
I miss him every moment of every day
I miss him ALMOST as much
As I miss her
My mother

G: Okay, gorgeous, I think that's enough of your blathering.

M: It's a holy day—we gotta get home. Get dressed up for church.

L: Yeah, today we're just gonna shoot you and go home. No torture today. No story today. We're exhausted from rounding up Muslims and killing them.

She laughs.

G: What's so funny?

ELEKTRA: Nice try, gentlemen. But you know what the furies have decreed— my fate is to be tortured and killed by you daily until I am somehow redeemed, and your fate is to listen to my story over and over and over before you torture and kill me. WE are all being punished by the furies.

M: I sometimes wonder which is worse.

G: Aren't you sick of telling it? We are sick to DEATH of hearing it.

ELEKTRA: I am hoping that telling it to the right people will set me . . .

L: Free?

G: Free?

M: Right. DREAM on, baby. None of us will ever be free.

Music. The men exit. ELEKTRA *turns to* CASSANDRA *on the other side of the stage.*

ELEKTRA: And so: please meet Cassandra, the beauteous prophet whom no one believes.

Scene Three

CASSANDRA: Me? Yes, well, I was a so-poor girl in a so-poor town in Russia living in a two-room apartment with my grandmother and my crazy uncle and my mother and three loud and ugly brothers—it was cold all the time because we couldn't pay heat; I slept in the same bed with my mother and grandmother—the food was bread and soup and many days nothing at all and where we lived was where they did nuclear bomb testing—everybody dead by forty in that place, babies born deformed. I did not want to throw away my life here so at the café my good friend Alusha, she told me these men from Slovenia—a most beautiful country; she showed me the pictures on the café computer—she tells me they are looking for girls, girls to be tour guide, to the tourists. I say well yes, I can speak English pretty good; I say yes, yes, I can send money back to my mother. So Alusha, she called up the man and he said we must pack up our bags that night and they took us away in the car and we travel for days to this country and it was all a deception.

I was a smart girl, yes, but I was only sixteen.

Oh, did you know?

I am royalty! Oh yes my baba, she told me long time ago, before the revolution, our family was high and this is a royal ring. See how it SHINES? It gave me the second sight from my royal ancestors. I am . . . what do they say in America . . . teller of fortune. Psychic? But it sounds cheap, no? In America they are mostly hustlers, con artist, and in Europe they are gypsies, trying to feed their children! Yes, it gave me the gift that I hate, which is to see what will happen. I look at a man, I know how and when he will die. I look at a building, I see the fire that will destroy it. But problem is? Because my grandmother was so angry for me leaving, she put a curse on my gift, that nobody believe me! So I stop believing in my own sights, you know what I am saying? Even though in my belly I did not trust these men, I wanted so much to get out that I told myself I was wrong. When we arrived in this place, in this crazy burned-out city, I said this does not look like the pictures, what is happening here? He say there is a WAR here, stupid, did you not KNOW there is a war? Do you not watch television? Look at news on your computers? Have you not heard of Sarajevo, of Croatia, or Bosnia? I say I am teenager, I don't look at news, don't care about news. Why you did not TELL us? He gave me a smack in the head, a punch in the face; he broke my arm and kept Alusha and I in a cage. YES, a cage, a crate for the big dogs, and then when our spirits were broken down, we were made to be . . . well of course you can guess. You are smarter than we were; you know the ways of the world. We did not. AS poor as we were, we were innocent. And so. Overnight—

We became . . . whores . . . for officers, because Alusha and I we are beautiful, and well-mannered; the low soldiers, they just took any girl they wanted, twelve years old, and passed her around and then fed her to the dogs, but the officers, they were gentlemen (or that is what they pretended to themselves); they did not want to rape screaming and frightened girls— they wanted young ladies who would have a conversation afterwards. So they wouldn't have sins to tell to their priests— I hated every moment, of course, but I could pretend to save my life; couldn't you?

And though I knew death would be better than this, I wanted to live to TELL THE WORLD. To talk and talk and talk until I take my last breath.

I am wandering over the world telling my story, and searching, searching always for my mother.

Mother

Oh I weep
To think of my mother
I LONG
To hold my mother
To kiss her kind eyes
Inhale the smell of her hands
Her hair

I will never see my mother again

Scene Four

CASSANDRA and AGAMEMNON. He is lying on her lap. She caresses his hair.

CASSANDRA: My sweet man. You are so different than the others. I think it is time you told me your name. I want to speak your name.

AGAMEMNON: Agamemnon. You have not heard of me, sweet girl?

CASSANDRA: The great General Agamemnon?

AGAMEMNON: *(laughing)* When I am with you, I am just an ordinary man.

CASSANDRA: But . . . You seem so . . . sad.

AGAMEMNON: I am far, far from my family. And the blood, the screams, the destruction . . .

CASSANDRA: The war is terrible.

AGAMEMNON: . . . The siege of our beautiful Sarajevo, all those civilians shot while rushing for bread, and worst of all they are killing *all those Muslim men*, hundreds, every day, in Srebrenica.

CASSANDRA: Srebrenica? But I thought that was a UN-protected city?

AGAMEMNON: We thought so too. But the Dutch soldiers there are useless. They believe the lies they are told by Menelaus, and they accept gifts from him. Bottles of wine, for their wives, candy. They drink with him, while those boys are being murdered.

CASSANDRA: No, no, no! This must stop . . . did you say Menelaus?

AGAMEMNON: General Menelaus. Leader of the Scorpions. In wartime we are all monsters, but they are the worst monsters.

CASSANDRA: I know General Menelaus!

AGAMEMNON: He comes here? To you?

CASSANDRA: Oh. No, not to me, baby, you are the ONLY one for me, but to my best friend, Alusha, next door. I hear him through the wall, crying, crying that he will go to Hell, that he is heartsick about killing those men and boys.

AGAMEMNON: THAT I do not believe for a second.

CASSANDRA: He has five boys of his own, his conscience is shattering him!

AGAMEMNON: He has no conscience. I should know. Menelaus is my older brother.

CASSANDRA: Your brother! But how is it . . .

AGAMEMNON: There are many brothers on different sides here. We are both Serbs, but I am a general of our Yugoslav Army, and I married a Muslim woman. He is head of the extremist Scorpion killers. I believe in the Geneva Convention; he—he believes only in killing.

CASSANDRA: Ahh but you men show women sides of you that no one else sees. Even a brother. Especially after making love. We see your soft side. The boy underneath the mask of the man.

AGAMEMNON: There is truth in that. You are very insightful . . . For a pretty little whore.

He smacks her bottom.

CASSANDRA: *(slaps him)* What? What did you call me?

AGAMEMNON: I am sorry. You are more than that, Cassandra . . . and I think it frightens me. Forgive me?

CASSANDRA: The point is, lover, he wants to make a DEAL!

AGAMEMNON: A deal?

CASSANDRA: You have occupied Sokolac, yes?

AGAMEMNON: Oh yes. Sokolac is mixed, like Sarajevo; I will not let him go in with his Scorpions and . . .

CASSANDRA: Listen! I hear him say to Alusha that if only you would give back to him the city of Sokolac he would stop killing the men. Immediately.

AGAMEMNON: Are you a spy?

He grabs her roughly.

CASSANDRA: No! NO! I swear on the life of my unborn children!

AGAMEMNON: . . . Yes, very well. One look at your eyes and I know you are telling the truth.

CASSANDRA: He is LOOKING for a reason, I tell you!

AGAMEMNON: He did say something about it before, but I thought he was bluffing.

CASSANDRA: Save those men. Give him Sokolac.

AGAMEMNON: What's in this for you?

CASSANDRA: I have brothers. I had a father. I care about those men, just as you do.

AGAMEMNON: Sokolac you say?

CASSANDRA: YES.

AGAMEMNON: Then Sokolac it is. Congratulations, Cassandra! You may have just brokered a peace! You may have saved many, many lives!

CASSANDRA: I have many talents, Agamemnon. Till this moment, you knew of only one.

Scene Five

CASSANDRA and MENELAUS.

CASSANDRA: My sweet huggy bear, your Cassandra has a solution to your problem!

MENELAUS: Ha! Come here . . .

CASSANDRA: Baby, you must listen to me!

MENELAUS: What would you know about war? You know the bed and the bed and the bed only!

CASSANDRA: My love, before the war I was studying political science! And I was a negotiator for our student union in Siberia!

MENELAUS: Ahhh. Brainy and beautiful, the most deadly! Smarter than me?

CASSANDRA: Oh NEVER, you are brilliant—you are my brilliant, and VIRILE, lord and MASTER

MENELAUS: Aghhhh. You are the sexiest . . .

CASSANDRA: Agamemnon has been here!

MENELAUS: What? My filthy, pathetic traitor brother? With YOU?

CASSANDRA: NEVER! You are my ONLY, you know that. After you, they are all boys. But he has been with my girlfriend Alusha in the next room. She said he cries for those men and boys every day, just as you do!

MENELAUS: I do not love all that killing. I am a human being and a father. But this is war. We cannot have them in our way, and we can never trust them; we must show them that this land is ours, and it is hopeless to fight for it. My brother betrayed us when he married that Muslim bitch, and now even further as he has become their protector. I will fight him to the end. They are STILL holding SOKOLAC, which we need to get to the sea; you think I LIKE seeing all those lives wasted? You think I am happy about that? Those boys are in my nightmares—you know I have five of my own.

CASSANDRA: My poor baby. You need a nice back rub. Oooh you smell so MANLY. I tell you the truth, he WILL give you SOKOLAC if you give back those Muslim men and boys safe. That is a promise; HE told Alusha that he would!

MENELAUS: You think I am going to negotiate based on whore's gossip? Even if you are my favourite whore.

CASSANDRA: Have I ever lied to you?

MENELAUS: No. I know how you worship me.

CASSANDRA: And you know how I feel about the killing.

MENELAUS: Yes. You have made that clear.

CASSANDRA: Just make the offer again, huggy bear. What harm can it do?

MENELAUS: *(kisses her)* You are too, too much. Unlike any other whore, you. I will arrange a meeting.

CASSANDRA: But you MUST keep your word to him! Those men must be safe!

MENELAUS: Hey! I have always been a man of my word. For you! For my five sons!

CASSANDRA: Kiss me. Again! Harder!

Scene Six

ELEKTRA: Poor Cassandra. Having to beg like a lapdog. And she was not begging for herself, but only for the lives of hundreds of men she would never meet, men who would probably kick her as soon as look at her.

But she was finally content, in a way, because she was finally doing something that mattered; she was more than a toilet for soldiers—she was a peacemaker.

That's the funny thing about what happened: I liked Cassandra. If I had a chance to meet her, we might have been best friends. After all, she loved my father in a way my mother never did.

But then, I never had any girlfriends. My mother said it was because I am too blunt; my father said they were jealous. My sister said it was because there was something . . . dangerous—

FURIES: DANGEROUS

ELEKTRA: —about me. And they could smell it.

I think it was because they could see my destiny. They could see the blood on my hands—

FURIES: BLOOD ON HER HANDS, BLOOD ON HER HANDS, BLOOD

ELEKTRA: —even when I was twelve years old.

I always longed, longed for a friend.

We are nobody—

FURIES: NOBODY, NOBODY, NOBODY

ELEKTRA: —if we don't have a friend.

And that's who I was.

Nobody.

Scene Seven

A meeting place: the original execution spot in the woods. MENELAUS
and AGAMEMNON, *with soldiers, bodyguards around.*

MENELAUS: I have to say, brother, I just don't . . . I don't fully trust you. It's too neat, too tidy. I think this may be a trick.

AGAMEMNON: I could say the same thing.

MENELAUS: But you NEED Sokolac because of the route to the sea, just as we do. I just don't believe you are going to give it up just so your five thousand peasants can live out their pointless lives.

AGAMEMNON: To me, their lives are sacred.

MENELAUS: Liar! I still don't trust you.

AGAMEMNON: What if . . . I offer myself.

MENELAUS laughs.

I will send my guards away, and I will be yours. If my men don't clear that town, you can chop me up into little pieces and then victory will be yours. Without a general our side will fall apart, and you are certain of victory.

MENELAUS: You are offering yourself? Hah! This is rich; imagine, my men dining on the liver of the great General Agamemnon . . . eating my brother's heart whole . . .

I don't know. If we have you, your army will come down on us; NATO would start bombing us; I don't think so. I don't think so.

I don't know, Agamemnon. I am starting to rethink your offer.

Give me a week.

AGAMEMNON: A week! But the men! Promise you will not resume shooting the men.

MENELAUS: I can't really promise that. This is war.

> *AGAMEMNON's daughter, IPHIGENIA, runs in with a camerawoman in tow, filming all of this.*

IPHIGENIA: Take me.

FURIES: TAKE HER, TAKE HER, TAKE HER

AGAMEMNON: Iphigenia? Good GOD what the hell are you doing here?

IPHIGENIA: I offer myself. Instead of my father.

AGAMEMNON: LEAVE NOW. This is NO place for you, Iphigenia! Go! Go!

IPHIGENIA: You cannot tell me what to do. Listen. General Menelaus—Uncle—I am more important to my father than his own life; he would never do anything to jeopardize my safety. If you have me you can be certain he will be true to his word. Take me.

FURIES: TAKE HER, TAKE HER, TAKE HER

AGAMEMNON: Stop! WHERE did you come from? You should be at home, with your mother, five hundred kilometres away! How did you—

IPHIGENIA: My spies told me what was happening here, Papa, and I AM a war correspondent for the journal you never bothered to read . . . and I will NOT stay at home while our country is being torn apart. You TAUGHT me to care, and I . . .

AGAMEMNON: Take her to the Green Zone.

(to guards) Right now.

IPHIGENIA: No. NO. Do not touch me. I am an adult, they cannot take me against my will. It is my choice to offer myself as collateral. I care about these men and boys being slaughtered daily. I want to stop it. I must stop it.

MENELAUS: I know your daughter is dearer to you than your own life. All the world knows about you and your family. It would be an . . . assurance.

AGAMEMNON: Please, Iphigenia. I beg you.

She goes to the soldiers.

IPHIGENIA: The world will say that I, a woman, ended the killing.

That A WOMAN was heroic. That A WOMAN sacrificed herself. One of the MANY thousands of BRAVE women in this war. You want to keep me all safe, a little girl, in ribbons and dresses? Father, I have SEEN the footage of those boys being executed. Five hundred every day. Boys of twelve and thirteen, crying, praying. Your army NEEDS YOU in command; you cannot do this. If our side falls then thousands more civilians will be massacred, thousands of young women raped to death . . . I'm doing this for my brothers AND for my SISTERS.

A long pause from AGAMEMNON; a huge struggle.

I am your PROMISE, Menelaus.

AGAMEMNON: If you do ANYTHING to harm my girl . . .

The fury of not just my army, but the WORLD!

MENELAUS: You know I never want to harm anyone. Especially not my niece, even if she is one of them. I am a peaceful man. As long as you do your part and give us Sokolac, your daughter will be a great heroine—she will receive the highest honours, be studied in all the history classes.

I want to take back Sokolac by nightfall. Do I need to say "or else," my dear brother?

AGAMEMNON: Within two hours, brother, it is yours.

Scene Eight

ELEKTRA: My noble sister; my noble, brave, and reckless sister. How could she have known that her blood sacrifice would lead to the destruction of our family? The killing of our father . . . A man with a pure heart, a perfect soul; he CARED about every one of those men and boys. After all, his children all had Muslim blood running through their veins. He intended to keep his side of the bargain—of course he did! And, at first, the clearing of Sokolac was happening just as he planned. His soldiers were leaving the town like perfect gentlemen, washing their own dishes, waving goodbye, all was orderly; SIX soldiers had been staying in the house of my cousins and great-grandmother, and as they were leaving, my great-gran—she was a little crazy; she had dementia; they had been keeping her quiet with pills, but of course they ran out of pills because of the occupation—and my great-gran, she hated the soldiers and swore at them as they were leaving; she threw a china plate, which hit a soldier in the head. He fell to the ground, his blood spraying out. His nervous friend shot my great-gran, and then, of course, my cousins attacked the soldiers with knives, and then the soldiers, of course, shot everybody in that house and the next house, and when my father arrived it was done. His soldiers had massacred 370 citizens of Sokolac.

Scene Nine

MENELAUS: *(weeping)* Aghhhhhhhhhhhh. These beasts, beasts! God forgive me, it is all my fault for trusting that DEVIL my brother!

He slaughters his own family now! Savages! I will show them what savage is: BRING HER TO ME.

Scene Ten

AGAMEMNON: *(opposite the soldier)* No! No. It isn't possible, no! What happened? WHAT HAPPENED, MAN?

SOLDIER: They lost their shit. When that old lady threw the plate, it was like a bomb went off—Vozik just SHOOTS, and keeps shooting—he's crazy, sir. I always thought there was something wrong with that guy—

AGAMEMNON: I want all the killers executed. Today. Now.

SOLDIER: Yes, sir.

AGAMEMNON is shaken, having trouble breathing. CASSANDRA embraces him.

CASSANDRA: Oh, I can feel it—they are dragging Iphigenia out; they are—

AGAMEMNON: Shut up! SHUT UP with that. I have ordered my men to storm the camp and pull her OUT of there. The helicopter is on its way for me. What the hell is taking it so long . . .

CASSANDRA: Oh, my love, I am afraid. I am so afraid for your daughter.

AGAMEMNON: Stop, just stop.

SOLDIER: Sir! The helicopter is just a kilometre away . . . we will . . .

AGAMEMNON clutches his heart, begins to collapse.

CASSANDRA: WHAT is happening? Agamemnon! Call the medics! Agamemnon is ill! Now!

Scene Eleven

ELEKTRA: My father's heart cracked . . . because of what had happened he had emergency surgery that day and so could not save my sister himself, so . . . he sent a team into the camp. He threatened, he pleaded—

FURIES: PLEASE

MENELAUS: Sorry, General Brother, this was your promise.

AGAMEMNON: I didn't say you could harm her in any way.

MENELAUS: Who said we will harm her? We'll keep her, that's all. Your five hundred men, though, they are already covered in maggots, feasting on their filthy flesh.

AGAMEMNON: She is just a young girl.

MENELAUS: Exactly.

AGAMEMNON: I beg you.

MENELAUS: I heard you were very ill. You have had heart surgery!

AGAMEMNON: Or I would be there now. My troops are on their way.

MENELAUS: They will never, never find us!

AGAMEMNON: I will kill you with my own hands.

Scene Twelve

MENELAUS: BRING HER TO ME!!

IPHIGENIA: I am here. So?

MENELAUS: A massacre.

IPHIGENIA: My father's soldiers?

MENELAUS: At his command.

IPHIGENIA: I don't believe you.

MENELAUS: Look at this.

He throws photographs on the floor.

IPHIGENIA: No! No . . .

MENELAUS: He broke his promise.

He shows her more pictures.

You see this woman? This is *our* grandmother—she brought me up; she is like a mother to me. See how they cut her throat?

IPHIGENIA: I know my father would never have sanctioned this. The perpetrators will be executed, this is . . .

MENELAUS: Your father's soldiers could not resist a killing field.

IPHIGENIA: NO.

MENELAUS: Or perhaps he ordered.

IPHIGENIA: No.

MENELAUS: You don't think he would give your life away like that?

IPHIGENIA: I KNOW he wouldn't. And YOU know he wouldn't.

MENELAUS: You know what this means.

IPHIGENIA: I do.

MENELAUS: Your father agreed. I am sorry.

IPHIGENIA: Don't worry. I'm not afraid. The gods are watching over me.

MENELAUS: One shot to the head. You will not feel anything. Just a white light, and you will no longer be. And your father will suffer forever.

The FURIES breathe fast, rhythmically.

Scene Thirteen

She is taken to the execution place from the beginning.

G: A woman?

L: We don't shoot women. Only THEY shoot women and children.

M: No, we rape them and hang them from the trees, don't we?!

G: Ha! Agamemnon's DAUGHTER. How sweet it is.

M: Boss said we had to shoot her. He said make sure it was in one shot.

IPHIGENIA: Are you religious?

G: Church every Sunday.

L: Beautiful Easter services.

M: I pray every night.

IPHIGENIA: And do you not believe in Hell?

G: Hell is where the enemy goes.

M: Hell is too GOOD for our enemies.

IPHIGENIA: Do you not believe this is sin?

G: You are the enemy. This is war.

IPHIGENIA: Shoot me. I will haunt you forever.

L: Get it over with so we can go home and watch the game. The NBA semifinals, man.

M: They always give us the dirty work—shooting a woman. I won't be able to look at my wife or my DAUGHTERS; it's my daughter's BIRTHDAY.

G: We could have some fun with her first.

L: You're disgusting.

M: THAT would not be right. Remember who we are.

G: Just some fun, hell she's probably dying for it.

L: If they find out we'll be shot.

G: They wouldn't give a shit and you know it.

L: Well. I guess . . . if really . . . If it's only fun . . .

IPHIGENIA: Your ancestors are watching you.

G: Oh. Didn't know the dead could see.

L: I believe in that.

IPHIGENIA: And every woman you have loved and cared for.

G: Wouldn't that be funny if that were true. But, baby, sad for you, it's not.

IPHIGENIA: They will know what you have done. I promise you they will know.

L: Just let's maybe cut her ankles soze she can't run, case we get too drunk.

IPHIGENIA: I will not run away. I am here as my father's daughter. I have chosen my fate. And I am NOT afraid.

G: We are gonna have some fun with you tonight, baby, gonna be an ALL-night run.

G ties up her hands.

IPHIGENIA: Whatever you do, I am not here. My body is here, YES, you have my body, you have this flesh, but I . . . am not. Here. I AM NOT HERE. You will never, ever touch me, understand? When you brutalize my body you know what will happen? My soul will explode and will THUNDER out my name and the names of every woman you and yours have murdered and will make lightning every time a woman is harmed.

YOU will never touch me.

G: I don't give a shit about any of that drivel. We aren't trying to touch your soul; you people have no soul, like animals, and that's why we can do anything we want to you and it's not a sin!

M: I'm outta here. You guys are sick.

G: Whatever!

L: Let the games begin.

L brings out a camera.

G: We can send our fun to General Agamemnon LIVE! Make him CRAZY!

THEN we deliver the body to MAMA by helicopter, dump her body on MAMA's front step!

Oh my God that'll be sweet, 'cause Mama gonna be MAD. Mama is not gonna let PAPA back in the house when she sees this. In fact, Mama is gonna be fit to KILL Papa. Ohhh this is gonna be good. Yuhyuhyuhyuhuippppppie!!!

IPHIGENIA: You will never touch me.

> *A highly choreographed slow-motion dance of horror:* CASSANDRA, *in her space, feels what is happening in her body.*

Strangely
Once the torture started
I was truly no longer afraid
I was outside of my body
Floating
And I reflected on fear
And I understood
What I was most afraid of
On this earth
Was not rape
Mutilation
And death
But where my real fear was
My raw
Primal fear
Was of
My sister
Elektra
Who had hated me since I was born
Since I took her place in my mother's affections
Her jealousy
Underneath her smiles
So much hatred
I could feel
She wished me dead
And now
Such a blessing from the gods

I forgave her
Fully
With all my heart
I only hope she will forgive *me*
For taking her place

ELEKTRA: I think I felt the moment that she died. I felt it in my hands—my hands began to burn.

> *FURIES start to sssssssss.*

They are still burning.

FURIES: *HAAAAAAAA*

IPHIGENIA: Through some heavenly mercy
The me-ness of me
The I-ness of I is not down there
But is hovering
Bright and burning and dancing above them
Like the northern lights
I have heard about the northern lights
I have WISHED for them
LONGED for them
And
Ahhh look at me now
I am
The northern lights

> *The murderers dump her body. The FURIES descend and destroy the soldiers.*

Scene Fourteen

FURIES: Break the window
Break the door
Break their backs
Hear us ROAR
You killers
Rapists
Woman-slayers
You are not safe anymore!
Just watch us!
Watch us flame
Watch us fire
We will haunt
Terrorize you
Feel our lightning strike you dead!

Three coarse breaths.

We weep oh we cry
For another broken angel
Broken
Battered
Butchered
Iphigenia

We will gather her in golden arms
Bring her to her mother
She who bore her
She who loved her

We are the kindly . . . avengers
With a treasure
At your door

They present the body of IPHIGENIA *to* CLYTEMNESTRA.

ELEKTRA *and* ORESTES *move in behind her. All three are in shock.*

Scene Fifteen

ELEKTRA: My father was gravely ill for a very long time
They had carried him to a safe place far away
A cave where Cassandra nursed him slowly back to health
My poor father had lost his mind
With the agony of knowing
What he had allowed to happen
He did not speak
He only rocked and rocked in the corner
His eyes fixed upon the ground
Together they stayed in that cave
For years
It was dark and so cold
His penance
He never left the cave
Cassandra only left occasionally to gather berries
And to work in the fields
In exchange for some milk and bread
And medicine
To help him breathe
To help him sleep
But my father's dreams were nightmares
Of the slaughter of my sister
Iphigenia

Scene Sixteen

CLYTEMNESTRA's home—we can see CLYTEMNESTRA mourning over the body of IPHIGENIA.

ELEKTRA: My mother.

She mourns for my sister day and night. She does not speak to me. She does not see me. She only prays. She watches the body like a loyal dog; she will let no one near it. And yes, I call it "it," because it is not my sister—it WAS my sister.

I will confess I was worried, when I heard of Iphigenia's death, that I might not ever feel grief, worse, that I might feel relief—because I have always been, I'll admit it, so jealous of her. While it is true that I did not grieve, I have not felt even a flicker of relief. I am human after all! And the jealousy has—actually vanished, can you believe it? Replaced with regret, that I didn't have the chance to be a better sister.

But I have given up on my mother.

Though I still crave her love, long for her gaze, yearn for her touch, her conversation.

She is no longer my mother. When I see her, I want to spit on her . . . I hate her.

Scene Seventeen

CLYTEMNESTRA *with the body of* IPHIGENIA

CLYTEMNESTRA: Iphigenia. Iphigenia, Iphigenia.

My dearest, dearest child, blood of my blood, my heart, my soul.

Where are your hands? Those hands that held my face, that moved like swooping birds whenever you told me a story, and your feet? When you were a child you walked on tippytoe, your heels never touched the ground, your feet soft doves.

Where are they?

And where is the flush in your cheek?

The way your cheek flushed when you spoke of your love, and his bravery, and when you showed me the necklace he gave you, with his name . . .

. . . Are you in there anywhere, Iphigenia? Is this body just a reminder of you? A symbol?

Or are you somewhere . . . In this slashed and broken body? Have you lingered in there just for me, my angel?

She cries, sobs, holds her.

My angel. I do feel; I feel your spirit, still lingering—your body just going cold, stiff. I will stay with you until you are soft again, until your body begins to rot, so I will know that your soul has flown—left the broken body; till I can see it in the air, like northern lights, flashing and colouring the air.

If it were not for your sister, your brother, I would join you, my Iphigenia; I would take you down to the lake and pull you in—we would swim together till the lake water fills our lungs and we become eels together, lighting up the dark sea, intertwined forever.

I will not bury you until he returns to see. For he must return; he will return to see your grave, to pray for forgiveness at your grave. And then I will show him what he has done. This: desecration.

CLYTEMNESTRA *turns to* ELEKTRA *and* ORESTES.

Let's each tell her what we remember, Elektra darling?

ELEKTRA: ahhhh . . . I . . . remember . . . ahhhhhh . . .

CLYTEMNESTRA: You must remember something—twenty-one years together . . .

ELEKTRA: I don't know . . .

CLYTEMNESTRA: She was your sister, surely you—

ELEKTRA: It's strange, as if she has always been dead.

CLYTEMNESTRA: Dear Elektra. You are in a state of shock.

ELEKTRA: We're in a war. People die. Every day. People who rush into the flames will be burned. I am angry at her, Mother. For leaving us, for . . .

CLYTEMNESTRA: I am sorry, my daughter. I have asked too much of you.

ELEKTRA: Yes.

CLYTEMNESTRA: I'm sorry.

ELEKTRA: But you always DO.

Pause.

CLYTEMNESTRA: I am sorry. Forgive me, my love. I know this is terrible for you as well. Orestes?

ORESTES: My big sister— She was like a goddess to me, seven years older than me, but always took the time to teach me the ways of the world, who to trust, and who to avoid; she sat me on her knee and answered all my questions, where do trees come from, how do they grow, why are there insects, and cats, and stars—she explained the stars to me, and time, and space, and speed, and age . . . and why men go to war, and why women suffer, and the death of my grandfather. She would talk and talk in such a soft and soothing way; she would sing . . .

(going to cry) I miss her laugh.

CLYTEMNESTRA: Nobody laughed like Iphigenia.

SERVANT: She always treated us so well, would pour me a cup of tea, and ask me about my family. I taught her how to make her favourite dishes, rhubarb crumble; we would spend hours in the kitchen, and . . . I just miss her. I miss her voice. Nobody had a voice like hers.

ELEKTRA: Like a crow.

CLYTEMNESTRA: Elektra!

ELEKTRA: Well, sometimes, when she was angry! Surely we are permitted some humour, some honesty.

CLYTEMNESTRA: Tell her. Tell her how you loved her.

ELEKTRA: I will not pretend—

CLYTEMNESTRA: TELL HER HOW YOU LOVED HER. She is still here, hovering, with her body.

ELEKTRA: You're crazy.

CLYTEMNESTRA: TELL HER.

ELEKTRA: I cannot say that.

CLYTEMNESTRA: TELL HER!

ELEKTRA: I hated her. We fought like alley cats—

CLYTEMNESTRA: Like SISTERS, darling, but that doesn't mean you didn't love each other!

ELEKTRA: I will not disrespect the dead by lying. I did not love my sister.

CLYTEMNESTRA: Your sister was tortured, Elektra, and murdered by a pack of savages.

THIS ISN'T ABOUT YOU.

ELEKTRA: BUT I AM ALIVE! She is dead, Mother, gone, and YOU! You spend all your time drooling over a dead body, like some demented dog. I'm sorry; I am sorry and I wish it had not happened, but really? She did it to herself. It's what she always dreamed of, being a MARTYR. The great martyr, Iphigenia.

But I am your daughter too, and I am still alive!

ELEKTRA storms out. CLYTEMNESTRA collapses.

ORESTES: Mama. She doesn't mean it. She's just so messed up—

SERVANT: I'll get her some tea, take her out to the garden—it always calms her to trim the roses.

ORESTES: She shouldn't have said those things! Mother, she is crazy, she always has been, don't listen to her.

CLYTEMNESTRA: You are a good son. Such a good son. Leave me now.

(to IPHIGENIA) Remember, remember when you wrapped my hair around your little fist, when you reached for me in the night; you had nightmares, so many nightmares: "Mummy! Mummy, Mummy, come! The bad man is chasing me through the woods, and the air is like mud I cannot run. I cannot run they are going to get me, Mummy!" And I would come to your bed and hold you close and tell you a story about fairies dancing in the meadows singing for the northern lights, and then the next morning we would go to the woods, pick blueberries and blackberries so you would see there was nothing to fear, and bake pies together, delicious, hot . . .

It's strange—before this happened, I had been having the same nightmare, about running through the woods, searching for my baby, but the air was like mud, I could barely move through it, searching behind every tree, asking the birds:

"Where is my baby? Where is my baby? Does anybody know where my baby is?"

CLYTEMNESTRA looks at the body.

Why? Why, why, why could it not have been me?

ORESTES: Mama, you need to rest.

CLYTEMNESTRA: You are such a good son.

CLYTEMNESTRA hugs ORESTES.

Scene Eighteen

CLYTEMNESTRA alone.

CLYTEMNESTRA: Agamemnon
Will you ever return?
Are you dead?
Alive?
How is it I could have loved
Kissed
Been one with
A man who would
Gamble with our daughter's life?
How is it I could have loved a man
Who is a shivering coward?
A cheat?
A killer?

What
Did war change you?
Make you a shadow of what you were?
Or did it reveal you
For the runt that you are?
What were you doing while your daughter was
Being tortured
And mutilated
And screaming for her father?
Drinking with the UN soldiers and dancing
While men and boys were being shot
And our daughter was hog-tied
Enjoyed
And then slaughtered like a pig

They took her hands as souvenirs
And her feet
But YOU CAN'T HAVE HER, DO YOU HEAR ME WHEREVER YOU ARE?
I HAVE HER
HER MOTHER HAS HER

War
Opens the door
To all that is . . .
Closed
In peacetime
To all but the
Freaks
Just as dogs in wartime move in packs
Become feral
WAR does this to men
Especially around women it
Lets their lifelong fear of ALL that is female
LONGING for all that is female
RISE UP
As HATRED
Without any consequence at all
With soldiers in wartime
Anything can happen
ANYTHING
He KNEW THIS
My husband knows the hearts and minds of men
At one time he was very wise
He knew the risk
He decided it was worth it

If he ever comes back
What will I say?
There is too much to say
And so I will say nothing
How will I look him in the eye?
I will never look him in the eye again

It will be a house of
Hatred
A house of
Silence
A house of death

FURIES: HAAAAA

Scene Nineteen

CASSANDRA: Agamemnon, my love, you are so . . . far away . . . today, please, tell me what is in your heart.

AGAMEMNON: It is time.

CASSANDRA: To leave this cave? Oh YES, I have been so HOPING you would say this!

AGAMEMNON: I am ready.

CASSANDRA: Ahhh. Yes. To go home, to your family.

AGAMEMNON: It has been years. I miss them, so terribly, especially my daughter Elektra. I can feel her missing me.

CASSANDRA: You are so brave.

AGAMEMNON: I am a coward. It is time to face the consequences of what I have done.

CASSANDRA: I hope they will forgive you. I pray!

AGAMEMNON: They will not. Why should they? But I must go down on my knees to them. I must show them the respect they deserve.

CASSANDRA: I will travel with you; you are still weak; I will help you.

AGAMEMNON: No. No, Cassandra. It is your time now; you must go home, to Russia; you must find your family.

CASSANDRA: My mother is dead; I heard she was shot by snipers when she tried to find me. You are my family now.

AGAMEMNON: Cassandra. I will never be able to thank you enough for what you have done—you have saved my life; you have nursed me through madness and sickness. I must go—alone.

CASSANDRA: Remember, no matter what happens, I love you. I know you only meant to save those men and boys and to one day rock your daughter's children on your knee. I know that.

AGAMEMNON: They will not. Every one of them will hate me, and rightly so. I will atone, atone for the rest of my life.

CASSANDRA: No. Not everyone will hate you. There is one . . .

(to audience) And so, we parted, forever. He went back to mourn for his daughter. And me? I wandered—through the burned-out villages, the valleys, the woods filled with wildflowers and, yes, dead bodies—so many dead bodies. For food I told fortunes to people—I held their hands and tried to tell them the truth, no matter how hard, and many times they would let me sleep on their floor, but I would always leave when the rooster crowed, for I was searching. I was searching all the time for my mother, for I felt in my belly she was alive, and searching for me also.

I am still searching for her, and I will not—I will not stop until I find her.

I would give the rest of my life to have one day, one hour with my mother.

Scene Twenty

ELEKTRA enters and stops in her tracks when she sees her father. Slowly she runs to him and throws her arms around him.

AGAMEMNON: My beautiful daughter.

CLYTEMNESTRA and ORESTES enter.

I want to see her. I want to see her grave. Is it nearby?

ELEKTRA: Oh yes. She is very nearby, isn't she, Mother?

CLYTEMNESTRA: Hush. Come with me, Agamemnon.

ORESTES: Are you ready for this, Father? It will be a shock. Are you sure?

ELEKTRA: Nobody could be ready for this.

AGAMEMNON: Are there flowers? She always loved roses.

CLYTEMNESTRA: Roses every day, my dear. White roses.

AGAMEMNON: Is she buried in the cemetery overlooking the sea?

CLYTEMNESTRA: No. We need to be alone.

ELEKTRA moves to go with them.

Closer than that. Come, my husband.

ELEKTRA glares.

Scene Twenty-One

AGAMEMNON: I thought you would never forgive me. I can certainly never forgive myself.

CLYTEMNESTRA: You did not kill her.

AGAMEMNON: My best friend. My conscience. I never in a million years thought they would . . .

CLYTEMNESTRA: They did
They sent me the video—
I heard her screaming . . .
I saw . . .
I saw her torture . . .
I could only pray ·
Pray for even a moment of kindness from the Scorpion brutes
But there was none!
There was NO kindness for our daughter
Whatever you imagined
It was a thousand times worse . . .
I cannot bear to keep breathing
Knowing what I know
I only go on for Orestes
And Elektra—

I was praying for your return, so we could share in our grief, for our family, for our baby.

AGAMEMNON: Where is she? Do you have her ashes in the vase she made for us, for our anniversary? The blue one, with the grey doves? I have imagined that . . .

He is alone for a moment.

Iphigenia.

CLYTEMNESTRA *appears with the skeleton of* IPHIGENIA *in a beautiful white nightgown.*

*She carries her in her arm*s.

CLYTEMNESTRA: She will never have to leave her home again
She will stay in her childhood bed until she is dust
She loved that bed
Remember
Agamemnon?
Because it is a sleigh bed
She said she felt like the queen of winter in that bed
I often sleep with her
Hold her until morning

AGAMEMNON kneels down.

When they dumped her body on our front step
She had been stabbed with bayonets sixty-seven times
I counted every stab wound
Is this too much for you?

Long pause.

. . . her fingers and toes had been cut off, as trophies, her hair pulled out; she was raped, of course, by dozens of men and by bayonet, by broken bottle, by gun. Unbelievably she was still alive when they were called to battle. They left her in the snow . . .

I saw her
Saw my baby in the snow
Reaching out

Calling out
Do you know what she said?

> AGAMEMNON *shakes his head.*

Do you want to see it?
Do you want to know what she said?

> AGAMEMNON *nods.*

"Don't leave me."

> *He howls from the very centre of his being, and collapses.*

Please don't leave me
Don't leave me here to die
I want to go home
I want to go home
I want my mother
I want my father
I want my mother

Please

Don't leave me
Don't . . .
Leave me . . .
Alone
Papa
Papa . . .

> AGAMEMNON *has trouble breathing.*

> *He collapses.*

> *He has a massive heart attack.*

CLYTEMNESTRA *watches.*

Agamemnon?
Are you having trouble breathing?
Agamemnon!
Aha
Agamemnon!
Answer me!
Are you . . .
You are clutching your chest
Is this . . . a heart attack?
Another?
Here
Take my hand
Try to breathe
Slowly
Just . . . try to breathe
Relax
She is at peace now
She knows you love her . . .
Is it very painful
You are turning blue
So blue
There is no oxygen in your blood now
Your organs are failing
Can you hear?
I think you can hear
I know you can
I am watching you die
What you have done
To your daughter has finally killed you
I have thought about this moment many many times
I have breathed revenge
And now the gods are with me
I will not have to suffer the consequences
Of killing you

I will live out my life a free woman
Free to mourn my daughter for the rest of my days
To bring flowers to her grave
Free
Finally of my feelings for you
My hate for you
Which began as a hot white ember
And grew and grew into a volcano
Always alive
Roiling with fury
Ready to erupt

I know she forgave you
Because that is who she was
But I cannot forgive you

But you have taken the easy way out
You are dying
Of a broken heart

Why hasn't it killed me?

    ELEKTRA appears. She sees her father is dead and rushes to his body.

ELEKTRA: Papa? Papa!! Oh my God. Mother? What happened to Father? What did you do? WHAT DID YOU DO? HELP! HEEELP!

    ORESTES enters and tries to revive AGAMEMNON.

Papa! Papa!

    ELEKTRA is wracked by violent sobs, the sound of a siren.

    The FURIES breathe a long exhalation . . .

Scene Twenty-Two

ELEKTRA: And so he was murdered by my mother
My father
The only person in the world who had ever loved me
Murdered
Dead
Forever

Because of her
Iphigenia

She took him with her
She wrenched my father from me
And my mother?
She killed him
She watched my father die
She took pleasure watching him writhing
Gasping for breath
She laughed
When I rushed in
He was dead
Cremated the next day
This is the vase
She gave it to me
She said:

CLYTEMNESTRA: Here is your father, Elektra. He is all yours now.

Scene Twenty-Three

ELEKTRA: Two thousand people came to HIS funeral, the great general. There was singing, and crying, and great speeches, and much sobbing.

I lived at home, with my mother and brother and the servants. I was hardly ever there, of course. When I was, we never spoke. I saw my father's death every time I looked at my mother.

Scene Twenty-Four

CLYTEMNESTRA appears, dishevelled, hungover.

CLYTEMNESTRA: Evening, sweetheart.

FURIES: Haaaaaaaaaaa . . .

ELEKTRA nods.

CLYTEMNESTRA: Been a while since we talked. How are things with you?

ELEKTRA: Not bad. You?

CLYTEMNESTRA: Well, you know, one foot in front of the other.

ELEKTRA: Yes. Me too. Have you been drinking?

CLYTEMNESTRA: So you've been . . . enjoying school?

ELEKTRA: Working with stone carving . . . yes. It's good.

CLYTEMNESTRA: Nice. You . . . like your instructors?

ELEKTRA nods.

Great. That's great. I'm happy for you, sweetheart.

ELEKTRA: Are you well? You seem so . . .

CLYTEMNESTRA: I'm tired, that's all. So tired.

ELEKTRA: I miss . . . him . . . you know?

CLYTEMNESTRA: Yes. Me too.

ELEKTRA: Really?

CLYTEMNESTRA: I did not want your father to die, Elektra.

ELEKTRA: Then . . . It must have been terrible for you . . . having watched him . . .

CLYTEMNESTRA: I was paralyzed, by shock.

ELEKTRA: His face must haunt you.

CLYTEMNESTRA: Every day.

> *ELEKTRA looks at her, pours a glass of wine for them both, puts poison in the glass for her mother, and hands it to CLYTEMNESTRA.*

FURIES: HA-HA-HA . . .

> *A series of breaths and the sound of punctuations . . .*

CLYTEMNESTRA: Well thank you.

ELEKTRA: I thought it was time we had a glass of wine together.

> *A beat while they drink.*

CLYTEMNESTRA: Oh. That is lovely.

ELEKTRA: This has made you so old.

CLYTEMNESTRA: Oh, yes, my bones are ACHING. I am getting old so fast. Look at my hair, like old straw.

ELEKTRA: Poor Mama, your hair used to be so beautiful.

CLYTEMNESTRA: A long, long time ago.

ELEKTRA: You know what I'd like to do? I'd like to wash your hair. I've got a lovely cream; it will leave your hair shiny, radiant.

CLYTEMNESTRA: Oh, Elektra! That will be wonderful. I love having my hair washed. It has been years.

ELEKTRA: I have it all ready for you. And I've sprinkled lavender in the water.

CLYTEMNESTRA: Lavender. You were such a sweet child, and now I am seeing that child again. My mother told me that I would. I love you so much. You know that, don't you?

ELEKTRA: Yeah. Yeah, I know that. I'm . . . sorry.

CLYTEMNESTRA: Oh, darling, sorry for what?

ELEKTRA: I've been such a . . . monster to you.

CLYTEMNESTRA: Well a lot has happened.

ELEKTRA: Still. I've been so hard on you.

CLYTEMNESTRA: It's what a mother expects . . . from her daughters. For a while, anyway.

ELEKTRA: Not Iphigenia, though.

CLYTEMNESTRA: It was different with her, she was always kind and sweet, but—restless—like a wild animal—from the age of fourteen—always wanted to be engaged with the world, out there, making an impact—that spirit . . .

ELEKTRA: That spirit of hers is . . . what killed her.

CLYTEMNESTRA does not respond, falls into thought.

I am so glad we are talking, Mama.

CLYTEMNESTRA: Yes. Me too.

Beat.

Ahhhhhhh. This is heaven. I love the fragrance of the lavender.

ELEKTRA: I'm so glad, Mama. You deserve a rest.

CLYTEMNESTRA: Tell me a story. You were always the best storyteller.

ELEKTRA: Me?

CLYTEMNESTRA: Oh yes. You used to entertain us with stories about a little mouse!

ELEKTRA: You remember that?

CLYTEMNESTRA: Wasn't his name Paxton?

ELEKTRA: Paxton the little grey mouse!

CLYTEMNESTRA: *(getting sleepy, slurring words)* Tell me, tell me the one . . . the one about when Paxton was in the garden and the children were—oh dear, I am feeling VERY sleepy, strangely sleepy, the mouses . . . were . . . having a very happy time . . . at . . .

CLYTEMNESTRA is losing consciousness.

SUCH a happy little grey—

He woke up before his twenty-six brothers and sisters and he tried to run, through the woods, but the air, was like mud . . . I can't run, I cannot find my baby, my baby is . . . where is my baby . . . my baby is . . . I love you, my girl.

As CLYTEMNESTRA speaks ELEKTRA pushes her mother's face down in the water. CLYTEMNESTRA, sleepy as she is, fights, kicking, and at one point almost flips herself out, soaking ELEKTRA, but ELEKTRA applies full force and lies over her mother in the bath, drowning her.

ELEKTRA is out of breath, gasping. Her mother floats. ELEKTRA lies on the floor.

ORESTES runs in.

ORESTES: Elektra!

ELEKTRA freezes.

What—oh my God. Elektra. What . . .

He rushes to his mother, pulls her out of the bath, gives her mouth-to-mouth resuscitation.

Mama! Mama!

ELEKTRA! What happened??

ELEKTRA: I don't know. I—

ORESTES: What the hell happened?

ELEKTRA: She was washing her hair— I heard a crash, I . . . I rushed in, and . . . she was having a kind of fit, a seizure . . . probably from all her drinking. I tried, Orestes: I tried but it was too late. She was under the water, and . . .

ORESTES is staring at her.

Long beat.

Orestes, she killed our father.

ORESTES: He had a heart attack!

ELEKTRA: And she watched.

ORESTES: He was dead within seconds, Elektra!

ELEKTRA: She killed him.

ORESTES: You are a murderer, Elektra.

ELEKTRA: I am a murderer, Orestes.

ORESTES: You will hang for this. And I will cheer.

ELEKTRA: Do you hear me, world? I killed my mother!

ORESTES: She was my mother too!

ELEKTRA: I killed my mother! I KILLED MY MOTHER!!

Scene Twenty-Five

The FURIES enter. A danse macabre.

They catch ELEKTRA as if they are weaving a web of torment.

FURIES: We are the furies!
She became lightning
CRASH!

ELEKTRA: I opened the door and I ran

FURIES: Across the night sky
Flash flash

ELEKTRA: I ran in my bare feet
Ran and ran until they were bleeding
Into the woods
I fell to my knees

FURIES: Like an animal

ELEKTRA: Like an animal

FURIES: Bleeding
Exhausted

ELEKTRA: I wanted to die

FURIES: WE ARE HERE
YOU ARE OURS
OURS

ELEKTRA: The furies descended
They picked me up in their sharp claws

FURIES: We flew her FAST

ELEKTRA: Out of time
Out of space

FURIES: To her punishment

ELEKTRA: INTO HELL

FURIES: This IS HELL

ELEKTRA: To endure

FURIES: What she endured

ELEKTRA: Night without end

FURIES: She wanted to die at last
Through muddy air we fly fast
Fly her to her penance
Until you find forgiveness

ELEKTRA: MY body tortured as

FURIES: Hers was

ELEKTRA: Night without end

FURIES: She is

ELEKTRA: Like a dream

FURIES: You are . . .
Ours

Scene Twenty-Six

ELEKTRA is tied up. The executioners from the beginning set up their shooting stick, joking around, taking their time, smoking cigarettes, and taking slow aim. L plays with his cellphone.

G: Hold on, hold on. I got an idea.

M: What now, smart man?

G: I wanna play a game.

L: You mean . . .

G: Yeah. That game.

M: Not that game again. It never . . .

G: Hey. You know how the story goes.

L: No, how does the story go?

G: She's gotta have a chance to save her soul, man. What's the POINT otherwise.

L: There is no point.

M: That's the point.

G: Okay, so, ELECTRIC.

ELEKTRA: Elektra.

G: I know, I know, I'm just kidding. You know my game?

ELEKTRA: No.

G: You gotta call her.

ELEKTRA: Who?

G: Her. You gotta shout out to her as loud as you can, over and over.

L: And if she hears you?

M: She will appear.

G: And the two of youse can go home.

ELEKTRA: WHO is SHE? WHO do you need me to CALL?

G: You know who.

L: We know you know.

M: Her.

ELEKTRA: Her?

M: The one who might come—when she hears your voice.

ELEKTRA: Oh. Her. She never comes.

G: Yes, her.

ELEKTRA: She will never come. She will never, never forgive me. Why should she?

M: There is always hope.

G: She might. Can't hurt to try . . .

L: You can trust him.

M: Maybe this time . . .

ELEKTRA: And this whole nightmare will be over?

G: You got it.

ELEKTRA: I will try. Once again.

L: Are you ready?

M: One, two. THREE!

> *They help* ELEKTRA *up to her feet—she is shaky—and walk her downstage.*

G: She's over the hill there somewhere—call her. Call her down.

M: Go on.

ELEKTRA: Mother!

> *She takes a deep breath.*

Motheeeeeerrrrrrrrrrrrrr

> *Another deep breath; she is exhausted.*

Mamaaaaa

> *She is crying, sobbing.*

Mamamaaaaa
Mama
Mamaaaa
Mamaaaa

She looks around. They all look around, laugh a bit.

G shoots her.

G: Dead?

M: Not quite.

G: So, I gotta get home. We're having another barbecue tonight. Beef brisket, my favourite. Only the in-laws are coming. My mother-in-law is such a . . .

L: Me? I'm watching the game.

M: I've got big money on it.

G: Your team is gonna lose, guys.

L: You are gonna eat those words.

He shoots her again in the head to make sure.

She calls again.

ELEKTRA: Mamaaaaaaaaaaaaaaaaaaaaaaaaa

CLYTEMNESTRA appears at the crest of the hill. She holds out her hand.

ELEKTRA sees her. Crawls to her. They embrace.

Epilogue

FURIES: Shall we forgive?

FURY ONE: As her mother has

FURIES: Set her free?

FURY TWO: As her mother wants

FURIES: Show her mercy?

FURY THREE: She has shown you her story

FURIES: You are her witness
Tis for you
Only you
Only you
To
Choose

Judith Thompson is a two-time winner of the Governor General's Literary Award for *White Biting Dog* and *The Other Side of the Dark*. In 2006 she was invested as an Officer in the Order of Canada, and in 2008 she became the first Canadian to be awarded the prestigious Susan Smith Blackburn Prize for her play *Palace of the End*. Judith is a professor of drama at the University of Guelph and lives in Toronto.

First edition: September 2017
Printed and bound in Canada by Imprimerie Gauvin, Gatineau

Author photo © Guntar Kravis

PLAYWRIGHTS
CANADA PRESS

202-269 Richmond St. W.
Toronto, ON
M5V 1X1

416.703.0013
info@playwrightscanada.com
www.playwrightscanada.com
@playcanpress

MIX
Paper from
responsible sources
FSC® C100212